The Indispensable Guide to End-of-Life Care

Also in the
Indispensable Guide
Series

The Indispensable Guide to Pastoral Care
by Shary B. Peterson

The Indispensable Guide to the Old Testament
by Angela Bauer-Levesque

The Indispensable Guide to God's Word
by Donald J. Brash

The Indispensable Guide to End-of-Life Care

Sharyl B. Peterson

THE
PILGRIM
PRESS
Cleveland

The Pilgrim Press
700 Prospect Avenue
Cleveland, Ohio 44115-1100
thepilgrimpress.com

Library of Congress Cataloging-in-Publication Data
Peterson, Sharyl B., 1951–
    The indispensable guide to end-of-life care / Sharyl B. Peterson.
        p. cm.
    Includes bibliographical references (p.   ).
    ISBN 978-0-8298-1848-2 (alk. paper)
    1. Death – Religious aspects – Christianity. 2. Terminally ill – Pastoral
counseling of. 3. Church work with the terminally ill. 4. Pastoral care.
I. Title.
BV4338.P47 2010
259′.4175–dc22   2010033705

1   2   3   4   5   6   7   8   9   10   15   14   13   12   11   10

Contents

Acknowledgments

First and foremost, heartfelt thanks to the love of my life and my very best friend — Bob. On my desk sits the card you gave me when I began my first book. On the front is a glittering, bejeweled fairy and inside is your message: "Together we can do it." And so we have — and do. Laughing, struggling, living, loving. Special thanks for all those early-morning horse-feedings and late-afternoon pen-cleanings you did so I could have an extra half hour to write.

Thanks and hugs to my four-legged fur-children. To Tilly and Jasper, my main and back-up writing dogs, and to Bella and Red Hawk, whose horse-energy feeds my spirit.

To my friends and colleagues Dr. Laurel Jones, the Rev. Dr. Melanie Porter, and Pastor Dan Wilkie, who read drafts of the manuscript and offered thoughtful, grace-full, and helpful comments. This is a far better book because of your insights, and I am a far better pastor and person because of your friendship, counsel, and support.

To all those who so generously gave of their time and shared their stories of caregiving, especially to Mike Blackburn (Callahan-Edfast Mortuary), Melanie Porter (Director of Spiritual Care, Hospice), John, Linda, and Susan (who asked that their last names not be used).

To everyone at Pilgrim Press who has supported my work in so many ways, especially to Timothy, Joan, Kim, and Tiffany. Also to John Eagleson for getting this whole thing into beautiful final form and print.

Finally, to all those patients and parishioners, both those still-living and those now departed, who have so graciously let me share the tenderest and most sacred moments of your lives. You have been my best, greatest, and most loving teachers.... This book truly is yours. Thank you for everything you have so graciously shared with me.

Chapter One

Pastoral Care at Life's End

While he was still speaking, some people came from the leader's house to say, "Your daughter is dead. Why trouble the teacher any further?" But overhearing what they said, Jesus said to the leader of the synagogue, "Do not fear, only believe." He allowed no one to follow him except Peter, James, and John, the brother of James. When they came to the house of the leader of the synagogue, he saw a commotion, people weeping and wailing loudly. When he had entered, he said to them, "Why do you make a commotion and weep? The child is not dead but sleeping." And they laughed at him. Then he put them all outside, and took the child's father and mother and those who were with him, and went in where the child was. He took her by the hand and said to her, "Talitha cum," which means, "Little girl, get up!" And immediately the girl got up and began to walk about. . . . At this they were overcome with amazement. He strictly ordered them that no one should know this, and told them to give her something to eat.

— Mark 5:35–43[1]

Overcome with Amazement[2]

On Christmas Eve, 1993, I was hospital on-call chaplain for the first time in my first unit of Clinical Pastoral Education (CPE). As the newest student in the CPE group, I had drawn the much-unwanted Christmas Eve and Christmas Day shift. That night, after attending to several minor incidents, I lay fully clothed on the cot in the on-call room as midnight was approaching.

1

I also lay there utterly terrified. I knew that deaths frequently occurred during the late-night hours, as did terrible accidents. I had never seen a badly injured person, much less a dead person, much less tried to care for them or their distressed families. I had no idea what to say or do and lay there rigid with fear that my pager would buzz and I would be summoned to deal with a situation that was painful and terrible and utterly beyond my ability to handle. I prayed fervently, "Please God, don't let anyone die on Christmas Eve."

At twelve minutes before midnight, my pager shrieked — and I nearly fainted with fear. I stumbled down the dark hallway to the elevator, and tried to remember how to get to the oncology unit. When I found it, the nurse on duty told me the room number of the man who had died and said that his wife was sitting with the body.

It took every bit of courage I could summon to walk down the hallway, knock softly on the door, and enter the room. On the bed lay an African American man who looked to be in his early seventies. His skin was the color of latte, his face freckled and waxy-looking. His intubation tube was still taped in place.

Next to the bed, a much younger woman sat holding his still hand and weeping. She looked up at me through her tears. I introduced myself as the chaplain, wondering if perhaps she was his daughter, rather than his wife. I stood there having no idea what to say or do next. I still don't remember many of the details of that night, except for meeting the man's children, all adults in their thirties. All of them clearly resented the young woman who had replaced their mother in their father's life, and I tried to help them sit and talk together without savaging each other. Somehow, and only by God's grace, we all survived the evening, and I may have managed to help them, even if only a little bit.

Thus was I baptized into the world of end-of-life care — and a very special world it is.

Some Basic Terms

In order to reflect together on this kind of care, it helps to have a common vocabulary to talk about its nature and about those to and with whom we offer such care.

* **Caregivers** are those who offer care, via their professional role or otherwise. In this text the term will usually refer to pastoral caregivers, those who offer care in the context of their role as religious professionals.

* **End-of-life care** refers to care offered to persons struggling with life-threatening illnesses, to those in the process of dying, to those who love them, and sometimes to other caregivers also involved in the dying process.

* **Dying** refers to the process of leaving this life and moving to the next. It is often complex and lengthy, and it involves a variety of physical, psychological, and spiritual changes on the part of the person engaged in that process.

* **Death** refers to the cessation of physical life. While we all begin to die the moment we are born, I will refer to those who are imminently going to die as **dying persons.**

* A **care-receiver** or **care-seeker** is anyone who seeks or receives pastoral care.

* **Strugglers** are those who are emotionally connected with the dying person, since they are typically struggling physically, emotionally, and spiritually with the fact of their loved one's death. They may be biologically related to the dying or deceased person, be part of that person's family of choice, or have other kinds of relationships. When their loved one is gone, they are **bereaved.**

* Those who experience loss also experience **grief,** a complex set of physical, emotional, cognitive, and behavioral responses. All persons experience grief after a loss, although they may experience or express their grief differently. In addition to these

feelings, they may also **mourn,** which involves public expression of their grief, often in the form of a funeral service or other ritual.

Common Concerns of
End-of-Life Pastoral Caregivers

Like me on that long-ago Christmas Eve at the hospital, many of my pastoral care students are fearful about offering care in end-of-life situations. When asked what part of pastoral care they are most looking forward to and what they have the most apprehension about, almost all students express concerns or fears about dealing with those who are dying and about helping their loved ones. Other emotions they often share are discomfort, anxiety, worries about being inadequate in the care they offer, and helplessness.

Before we go on, I invite you to stop reading here and spend some time reflecting on some questions. What experiences, if any, have you had with dying people? How were those experiences for you? What feelings did you have? Where did those feelings come from (stories your family told, things you've seen on television, somewhere else)? How do you feel about your own death? About the deaths of others you love? How might these feelings affect your ability to help care-seekers to whom you pastor? When you think about working with people at the end of life, what is the strongest feeling that arises for you? What is the greatest concern you have? What is one gift you bring? After thinking about these questions, you may also wish to spend some time journaling about them or praying with them. As with every form of pastoral care, we begin from our own experiences, feelings, and sensibilities. The greater awareness you have, the more effective a caregiver you can be.

Feelings of apprehension, uncertainty, anxiety, and fear are natural and arise from several sources. First, for most people in the modern world, death is *unfamiliar.* Most people who enter ministry have had little experience with the dying.

As recently as 1960, most Americans died at home. Family members cared for them as they died, and they usually had time to say their good-byes to each other. When people died, their loved ones washed and prepared their body for burial. And before the spread of clergy to most communities, family members typically offered the burial prayers and conducted the funeral service.

Since World War II, with advances in technology and many social changes, the majority of Americans now die in hospitals. At the end of life they are cared for primarily by professional medical staff. Their bodies are prepared for burial or cremation by professional mortuary staff. Their funerals or memorial services are conducted by professional clergy. Family members no longer have intimate involvement with the dying person, but instead have become visitors and onlookers. So, death is no longer viewed as a normal part of the life cycle, but as remote, unfamiliar, and often frightening.

It may be helpful to remember that the people for whom you care will have as little experience with death as you do. They are more likely to have learned about death through films like *Wit* and *The Bucket List* than from personal experience. They will have viewed television coverage of war deaths, auto accidents, and horrific murders. They will have read newspaper reports of medical mistakes and medical miracles. But few have actually experienced the journey through the dark valley described in Psalm 23. They will look to you as their companion and guide on the journey and for hope that comes from faith.

A second source of many caregivers' worries or other strong feelings about end-of-life care has to do with *confusion between "curing" and "healing."* Many people enter ministry because they want to be healers, which may be why you are reading this book. The good news is that you are already able to offer healing. And the more caregiving you do, the more you learn, the better you will get. However, in many situations, including end-of-life situations, you may not be able to offer cure. And that's okay.

Curing is sometimes defined as "restoring to health." If a person with an illness is "cured," the problem or disease is eliminated.

Curing focuses on taking an action directed toward the damaged part of the body or mind, with the goal of repairing the damage.

Healing often involves restoring to health, but more importantly, it involves restoring to wholeness. Where cure tends to focus on the parts of the body that have "gone wrong," healing focuses on the person as a whole being — body, mind, and spirit. Healing may be accomplished even though the disease or harmful condition is still present. In fact, healing can take place despite not only illness, but even death. While cure may be impossible, healing can almost always occur. As a pastoral caregiver, you can help that healing happen.

A third, and related, source of caregivers' concerns that may be especially acute in end-of-life situations is many ministers' *fears that they are "not enough."* If they are unable to cure, or to fix whatever is amiss, they may feel they shouldn't be involved in such care. Or, in a culture that tells everyone that with enough effort you can do anything, they may exhaust themselves trying to accomplish the impossible.

A related worry is the sense of being an "imposter." Some caregivers are uneasy about whether they are really welcome in pastoral-care settings or are imposing on others, and whether they really do have the skills and faith needed to do this work.

The important point here is that your presence alone goes a very long way toward being "enough." We'll talk more about presence later, but the fact that you are willing to be with the person who is dying, suffering, or bereaved matters more than you can imagine. Your willingness to sit and hold someone's hand when everyone else has abandoned that person, or to listen to someone's pain when no one else is able to, makes real in powerful ways the fact that God is indeed with them. And whether or not our own skills and knowledge are completely "adequate" (and perhaps they never are), God always is. The One who created us and loves us is always enough. And this loving, caring God will help caregivers be enough for those who need them.

A final source of deep feelings about end-of-life situations includes *experiences* you have had with, and *messages* you have received about, death and dying from your own family, or from the wider culture around you. If you have had positive experiences — say, the death of a sibling in which you were lovingly included and helped to say good-bye — you are more likely to be comfortable being with someone who is dying or with someone who is grieving. If you have had negative experiences — like being with a loved one who suffered greatly in the dying process — it may take longer for you to become comfortable in these settings.

Current popular culture sends mixed messages about death. On one hand, we are told that death should be avoided at all costs. If people eat right, keep their bodies in the condition of a twenty-year-old's, drive the right car, and so on, death can be avoided — or at least postponed as long as possible. At the same time, our culture has become more accepting of death than ever before. News coverage of widespread death from wars, natural disasters, or famines raises only minor public concern or outcry. Deaths in our own communities from homicides, child battery, or causes related to poverty are increasingly accepted as being part of "the way things are."

Any or all of these communications may have created emotions about the end of life of which you may be unaware until you encounter a particular caregiving situation. It will help you and your future care-receivers if you spend time now examining and reflecting on the messages you have received, and what your current beliefs are about death and dying.

Biblical Understandings of Death and Dying

The messages faith offers about death are usually very different from those just described. They are also much more helpful in our pastoral caregiving. So what does the Bible have to say about death and dying?

First, it offers diverse understandings of death. Physically, Scripture understands death as a limit built into the human biological condition. We live in bodies, and at some point those bodies stop functioning. So, mortality and human finitude are not viewed as evil but simply as part of what it means to be a human being.

Spiritually, death has to do with separation from God or from other people. Speaking heresy or inciting people to turn away from God were punishable by death, in part because such actions led to spiritual death for those involved (e.g., Deut. 13:5, 10). The numerous laws in Leviticus in which offenders are to be put to death (e.g., those who blaspheme, those who murder, those who transgress laws about family relationships and intimacy, those devoted to destruction, and so on) involve causing spiritual death through separation from other human beings.

New Testament writers expand this theme, as when Paul states that hostility or disobedience to God leads to spiritual death (Rom. 8:6–9), and when the writer of 1 John reminds the faithful that those who do not love their sisters or brothers "abide in death" (1 John 3:4). Life, we are told, is about relationship and connection. Death is about separation and disconnection, from our Source and from our fellow creatures.

Second, the biblical writers wrestle with the relationship between death and the human spiritual condition. In the Hebrew Bible, death is linked to human sinfulness. In the Creation story, God threatens Adam with death if he disobeys God by eating from the tree of knowledge of good and evil (Gen. 2:17). And when Adam and Eve disobey, part of their punishment includes eventual death (Gen. 3:19). This connection between sin and death reappears throughout the Hebrew Bible, where "suffering and death [are] construed as divine punishment for violation of covenant (with God) or of the (intended) moral order of creation."[3]

Even in progressive faith traditions today in which this view has largely lost credence, echoes of such beliefs may resonate for some care-receivers. It will be beneficial to reflect on your own biblical and theological understandings in this area so you can be centered and pastorally helpful if such concerns arise for those to whom you offer care.

In the Greek Testament, understandings become even more complex. On one hand, Paul reiterates the ancient view that death is an enemy and is punishment for sinfulness, as in his much-quoted "the wages of sin is death" (Rom. 6:23). On the other hand, life emerges as the predominant theme of human existence.

In particular, humanity has received new life in Jesus Christ as Paul goes on to say in the rest of that quotation: "but the free gift of God is eternal life in Christ Jesus our Lord." This new life is spiritual, and occurs both in the present world and in the world to come. That does not mean that biological finitude has been overcome and that people will no longer die physically, but rather that bodily death is not the final word.

Most Christians believe that God has acted through Jesus Christ to assure final victory over death and that Christ died that humankind might live. Jesus Christ is "the resurrection and the life and those who believe in [him], even though they die, will live" (John 11:25). Thus, through his resurrection believers too are granted eternal life. The concept of "death," then, takes on a new meaning: existence without salvation in Christ. Finally, at some time to come, "Death will be no more; mourning and crying and pain will be no more" (Rev. 21:4).

As with so many other aspects of the human condition, the Bible helps us appreciate the multidimensionality of death. Clearly, it is not simply something that happens when a person ceases to breathe. Rather, it can occur on different levels of existence. Yet people of faith can face it confidently and with hope, certain of the grace of God in Christ. Even so, as we shall see, they may struggle when death nears.

Pastoral Care at Life's End

The word "care" comes from the Gothic word *kara*, which means "to journey with" or "to be with." Pastoral care involves journeying with others in a way that grows out of and is grounded in our deepest faith commitments.

What makes care explicitly "pastoral" is that it *involves a relationship that intentionally and knowingly involves three partners: the caregiver, the care-seeker, and their God* — in other words, it is care that has explicitly theological roots and explicitly theological nature. Because God cares for humankind, human beings are called to care for one another. When caregivers invoke that relationship as a foundation for their caring, and when they intentionally invite God into the care process, they are offering "pastoral" care.

For those in end-of-life situations, theological questions often take on new salience and urgency. For example, while most people occasionally wonder what existence is like after we leave this world, that question takes on new importance when you are imminently facing the loss of your own or your loved one's life. We will consider this further in chapter 3.

Another fundamental element of pastoral care is *presence*. Presence means being there with the care-receiver — being there physically and being there mentally and spiritually. It is not a matter of doing or saying the "right" thing so much as being attentive to them, focusing on them and their needs, at that point in time. We will consider this in more detail below.

In order to be really present to another person, you must have a high level of *self-awareness*. You must be conscious of your own attitudes, preconceptions, and biases, about people, situations, and life circumstances. You must have strong, healthy boundaries. And you must practice good self-care, a topic we'll explore in greater depth in chapter 4. These are essential qualities to develop and nurture in all forms of pastoral caregiving. They may be especially important in end-of-life care, which involves unique physical, emotional, and spiritual demands.

You must also be able to *accept limits*. When someone is dying, presence takes on a special form. It often means admitting your helplessness to make things all right, or even better. It means being willing to sometimes simply sit and bear witness to another's pain. As a caregiver, you must learn to accept your limitations, to offer what care you can, and leave the rest up to God. God has the answers you do not, and ultimately what happens is in God's hands. If you can trust that, care-receivers may be able to as well.

End-of-life care-receivers also, perhaps more than at any other time, need caregivers who can *"hear them into speech."* This phrase, coined by Nelle Morton,[4] refers to the role of the caregiver in helping care-receivers tell their stories and in the process, make clearer to themselves, to the caregiver, and to God, their needs, desires, and hopes. This is done through the practices described above, as well as by framing your questions and comments in open-ended ways that permit and encourage care-receivers to express themselves and to become more aware of their deepest feelings and concerns. You also facilitate this by listening theologically, helping care-receivers to link their own situations, feelings, and hopes to those of our ancestors in faith, and helping them bring those things most important to them to their God and ours.

Presence

The single most important gift you can offer care-receivers is your presence. That means being with them physically, intellectually, emotionally, and spiritually, focusing on them and their needs and not on your own worries or anxiety about doing the "right thing," and truly listening to them and their stories.

Presence is not about accomplishing something, about fixing the other's pain, or about offering solutions. It is not about expecting them to feel or act any particular way or to achieve any particular goal in their journey toward the end of this life. Presence is about being willing to simply walk alongside them.

Alan Wolfelt and Greg Yoder, in their exceptional books *Companioning the Bereaved*[5] and *Companioning the Dying*,[6] respectively, refer to this kind of presence as "companioning" others. Key tenets of the companioning process include a holistic approach that honors all aspects of the person — his or her physical, emotional, cognitive, social, and spiritual being. This focus involves a balance between the past, present, and future and respect for the expertise of the care-receiver — that they are the authority on their experience.

Perhaps most significantly, "companioning is about going into the wilderness of the soul with another human being; it is not about thinking that you are responsible for finding the way out."[7] Companioning means recognizing that the journey is theirs, and while it is important for you to accompany them, you are not in charge of the trip, nor required to make sure it takes a specific direction or form. You are there to remind them that God is traveling with them.

The Communal Context

In the story from Mark's Gospel with which this chapter begins, we see a community in action. Jesus is teaching. The leader of the local synagogue is in the audience. Several people come from the leader's house to inform him that his little daughter is dead. Jesus immediately takes several of his followers along with the bereaved father and goes to the house, which is surrounded by yet another group of people, already wailing and mourning. He enters the house, where more people are mourning, goes alongside the dead child and her mother, and raises the child to life.

In Jesus' world — in fact, in most of the world of the Bible — community was central to life. From birth to death, one was surrounded by people, and one was a part of others' community. Behavior was always understood in terms of its effects on others. Rules were made and faith teachings exhorted with the goal of benefiting the common good. We have lost much of that sense of community in today's world, with pastoral care typically construed as an interaction between one pastor and one care-receiver (or family of care-receivers). It is important to recapture that communal orientation when offering end-of-life care.

In part this is because care for the dying, perhaps more than any other form of pastoral care, often involves partnering with other caregivers. They may include other spiritual-care providers (e.g., hospice or hospital chaplains), health-care providers (doctors, nurses, hospice team members, psychotherapists), family members, and social workers. End-of-life care also nearly always involves family members of the dying, including spouses, partners, parents, adult children of dying parents, and others.

For pastoral caregivers, it is important to remember that you are only part of the community of care. This is good news, because it relieves you of the sense of total responsibility for the well-being of those dying, of strugglers, and of the bereaved. Not only are you partnering with God in the care you offer, you are also partnering with other people.

In addition to those listed above, special support groups (e.g., for men who have breast cancer, for parents of children with AIDS) may offer a level of understanding or feelings of validation that you cannot. Most communities offer such groups through their hospitals or social service agencies, and more and more churches are starting such groups.

Another reason that community is so salient in this discussion is that care for the dying and the bereaved is shaped in significant ways by the care-receiver's social location,[8] particularly by the care-receiver's ethnicity and cultural background. Persons from different backgrounds have different sensitivities to, concerns about, and preferences regarding issues that vary from medical procedures that may be used to sustain life artificially to appropriate ways to express grief to burial practices. It is essential for caregivers to be sensitive and responsive to the issues and concerns raised by this reality.

Thus, end-of-life care is necessarily communal in nature. It is shaped by the communities of which both dying and bereaved persons are a part, as well as by the community of caregivers involved at the end of the dying person's life. The pastoral caregiver is one member of this community and needs to be sensitive to all the rest. This text is designed to help you learn how to do that.

Chapter Two

Loss and Grief

For everything there is a season,
and a time for every matter under heaven.
—Ecclesiastes 3:1

Death out of Season

A hospital chaplain was paged to the E.R. late one Monday evening. The admitting nurse directed him to a small group of teenagers huddled together in the waiting-room, crying. As he sat with them, he learned that Maxie, a sixteen-year-old girl who was a friend of theirs, had just died.

They had been sharing a ride to their night jobs at a fast-food restaurant, laughing and joking with each other as usual. Suddenly Maxie, who was sitting in the backseat, fell over, her eyes closed, and apparently unconscious. They had the good sense to head straight for the hospital, where she was placed on a gurney and immediately taken into an exam room. Only minutes before the chaplain arrived, one of the E.R. doctors came to tell them she was very sorry, but their friend hadn't survived. Apparently, despite Maxie's youth and apparent good health, she had had a heart attack. Her buddies were terrified, confused, and devastated by the sudden and completely unexpected loss of their friend.

Loss Is Part of Life

While this book focuses on some of the hardest losses in life, it is important to remember that loss itself happens all across the life span, from the time we are babies until the end of our time on earth arrives. As children hear the word "no" from others, they lose their sense of omnipotence. As they enter school, they lose some of their freedom as they adjust to rules and the presence of many others in their lives. As teens or young adults, they lose their friends and sense of "home" as they move on to higher education or to new jobs. As older adults, they lose their belief that they can always protect their children, or that life is always fair. Loss is simply part of the human package.

When most losses occur, we grieve a little or a lot, mourn or not, adjust, and move on. When loss of life occurs, whether it is unexpected like Maxie's or is imminent for ourselves or for a loved one, the intensity of the loss may feel far greater and its potential to devastate far stronger. Persons experiencing these losses have a great need for care and support. Let us turn to some of the losses care-receivers experience and the implications of those losses for pastoral care.

The Experience of Loss[9]

To help you enter into the experience of those facing profound loss, quiet yourself and explore this exercise. Take a blank piece of paper. On one side, list the ten people, things, and activities that are most important to you in your life right now. On the other side, draw a target like that used by archers, with a center circle and three concentric circles around that. Next, review your list on the other side. Inside the center circle write the two items that are most important to you. In the next circle out, write the next three most important things. In the next circle out, write the two next most important. In the outer circle, write the last three items.

Now imagine that you become ill — say, with flu serious enough to interfere with your normal activities and relationships. Put an "X" through one or two items in the outermost circle that you imagine losing. As you mark these out, and each time below that you eliminate items, notice what it feels like. Now, imagine that your flu gets worse, turning into a serious medical problem that necessitates a trip to the E.R. and extended bed-rest. "X" through the remaining outer circle item(s) and the two next inner circle items. Then imagine that the drugs you've been given don't help, and your medical problem becomes so severe that you are hospitalized for several weeks. "X" out one or two of the next inner circle items. Next imagine that you become so ill that you require surgery and continued hospitalization. "X" out all remaining next-to-inner-circle items. Finally, imagine your condition worsens to the point where your survival is uncertain. You remain in the hospital, extensively medicated, in great pain much of the time. "X" out one of the two innermost circle items.

Now sit back and take several deep breaths. Notice what you are feeling — in your body, in your heart, in your spirit. What did it feel like to eliminate items on the different circles? What psychological issues come to mind for you? What theological issues come to your attention? While this exercise can only hint at the experiences persons who are dying or who are struggling actually know, it does offer some clues about their possible feelings and concerns.

Losses for the Dying Person

The losses faced by each dying person will be unique, since every person's dying process is individual. Even so, there are many common losses faced by those who are dying.

Feeling well and being pain-free is something most well people take for granted. For many dying people, it is a condition unlikely to be regained, at least for any long period of time. They often feel weak from their illness or from the treatments they receive, with little strength to engage in normal activities. Thus, they also lose the joy and satisfaction they once derived from preparing a meal, washing the car, or writing a letter. And while new medication systems have greatly decreased the likelihood a person will suffer agonizing physical pain, it often is "still there, lurking around the edges, waiting to pounce," in the words of one woman dying from breast cancer.

Mobility may also be lost as the person grows weaker. He may be unable to walk without assistance. She may become too weak to sit up in a wheelchair. Over time, this may mean the patient is unable to leave the hospital or, if at home, is unable to join the family around the dining table or even leave the bedroom. With the loss of mobility comes the loss of independence.

A *sense of personal dignity* is lost, especially if the dying person is treated like a "case" or a set of symptoms. While greater sensitivity in the medical community makes this less likely today, patients still are subjected to procedures in which their bodies are exposed to the gaze of strangers, in hospital hallways, labs, and treatment rooms. When forced to wear hospital gowns, they lose the sense of dignity that well people take for granted when they can choose their own clothing and wear what is comfortable and friendly. If they are hospitalized, strangers enter and exit their rooms without their permission, sometimes when they are toileting, having dressings changed, or being examined.

Choices are often reduced as the sphere of the person's living contracts. The dying person may lose the ability to make wise decisions, due to effects of medications or of his illness. If treatment options have been exhausted, she may have no further choices about what treatments she wants or is willing to have. Over time, choices may be reduced to whether or not he wants the window-blinds left open or whether she wants apple or cranberry juice for breakfast. Because it is our thinking and decision-making ability that give human beings our sense of autonomy and personal power, this area of loss is one of the most devastating.

Relationships necessarily change over the course of a person's dying. A spouse or partner who once was the cared-for person in the relationship becomes the caregiver, costing the dying person her former role, or costing him his sense of independence and dignity as he is cared for by someone else. A carefree adult child may have to give up her roaming and settle down to care for a dying parent. The dying person's ability to be physically intimate with a spouse or partner may diminish, with the physical and emotional losses that brings. Caregivers may hesitate to touch the dying person, so they lose that fundamental comfort. Friends often stop visiting, due to their sadness, discomfort, or fear of saying or doing the wrong thing, leading to a sense of painful isolation. The dying person loses her hope of seeing her grandchild graduate, of traveling the world after retirement with his life-companion, of sitting on the back porch and growing old together. And they lose their sense of there being a future stretching ahead. As one dying person put it, "cancer means there are no more plans."

Losses for the Struggling

Just as in the process of dying related losses are unique to each person, so are those losses experienced by the people who love them, who may be caring for them, and who are anticipating, or have just experienced, their departure from this life. Even so, there are certain losses that many struggling people encounter.

Freedom, time, and *autonomy* will be lost if the struggler is also providing care for the dying person. Life is torn from its usual track, and work schedules, child-care, and recreation all may need to be reorganized around the care of the patient. "Normal life" is no longer about feeding the dog, doing the laundry, picking up some groceries, and doing one's work, but about medication and hygiene routines, medical appointments, and treatments. Caregivers may feel angry that "my life is not my own anymore."

Feeling well may also be lost by strugglers over time, as they become more and more exhausted and depleted emotionally, spiritually, and physically. It may be hard to convince them of the need to take care of themselves, as well as their loved one — yet it is important to do so.

Feelings of safety and security may vanish, especially in the case of a catastrophic end-of-life situation. For example, in the story at the chapter's beginning, Maxie's friends were devastated not only because they cared about her and were anguished by her death, but also because it was totally unexpected. Sixteen-year-olds are simply not supposed to die, healthy forty-year-olds are not supposed to have heart attacks while bicycling on Saturday morning, and no one is supposed to be gunned down on a city street where they are vacationing. When things like this happen, the survivors' sense of order and justice in the world may be severely damaged.

Relationships are also threatened, particularly the struggler's relationship with the dying person. The nature of the loss will feel different depending on the relationship between the struggler and the dying person. The loss of someone who is very close — a life-companion, child, or parent — is usually much more painful than the loss of someone more distantly related. A parent losing a young child experiences losses different from a parent who is middle-aged and loses an adult child; a child who loses a sibling experiences loss differently from an adult who loses a sibling. And a struggler who is losing someone with whom they have had a conflicted relationship will sustain losses different from a struggler losing someone with whom they have had a warm and loving relationship. Moreover, like the one who is dying, strugglers may experience a sense of isolation as friends and family members stop visiting or calling. And at least for a while they too may lose their sense of future possibilities.

Losses for the Bereaved

Those who lose loved ones experience these losses and more. Every level of life experience is assaulted, as grievers are diminished in their abilities to function cognitively, emotionally, physically, and spiritually. The bereaved lose their sense of *well-being*, of *emotional security and stability*, parts of their personal *identity*, their *rootedness and faith in the past*, and their belief in a hopeful and happy *future*. Regardless of their particular relationship with the deceased, they are in deep pain and in desperate need of knowing that God will somehow sustain them through it.

Special Circumstances

So far we have primarily been considering situations that fall within the normal scope of life. People age, grow ill, are sometimes

in accidents, and die. As painful as those deaths are for strugglers and the bereaved, there are also end-of-life circumstances
in which death occurs not only unexpectedly, but also due to circumstances that lie outside the normal orderly operation of the
universe. Each raises special issues of loss and grief.

For example, imagine a couple, enthralled with their beautiful new active, happy baby boy, who finds him dead in his crib
one morning. Imagine a couple whose teenage son commits suicide, or whose daughter dies from an overdose of drugs. Imagine
the man who receives a call late one night telling him that his
life-partner has been found murdered. In all of these situations,
the grievers' worlds are forever changed, and while they share all
the losses described above, they also experience some losses that
are different from those experienced by people facing other kinds
of loss.

These bereaved almost always feel *guilt*, and may fixate on what
they believe they could or should have done differently that would
have prevented the death. For example, parents who lose infants
to SIDS may go over and over where and how they think they did
the wrong thing — whether they should have bought a new crib
instead of a used one, or not left the baby with a sitter. The parent
who loses a child or the teen who loses a sibling to suicide may
agonize over what cues they missed, what they should have said
or done that they believe would have led to a different outcome.
Loved ones of homicide victims may believe that if only they
hadn't let the deceased go to that party, take that job, work in
that environment, their loved one would still be alive. In all of
these cases, rarely could the death have been prevented, but that
reality seldom prevents or heals the survivors' feelings of guilt.

Survivors may also experience *shame*, especially when deaths
are due to violence. When a person takes his or her own life, or
their life is taken by another, those left behind often have tremendous difficulty accepting that the death has in fact occurred. Even
when faced with the agonizing task of identifying the body, feelings of unreality may be paramount and then are replaced by
mortification.

Those who lose children may lose *their committed adult relationship* as well. Some studies estimate that as high as 90 percent of all bereaved couples face serious marital problems after the death of their child.[10] Although couples may have supported each other through the illness of a child, or through a child's emotional or behavioral difficulties that culminate in suicide, once death occurs, it is very difficult for them to support one another in their grief, because each one is suffering so deeply. Many of these marriages end in divorce after a child is lost.

Survivors' *relationships with God* may also be deeply affected. While those who are bereaved often struggle with questions about where God is in the death, that uncertainty is even more pronounced for those whose loved ones have died "unnaturally." Kenneth Czillinger studied parents who had lost children to SIDS, to illness, and to suicide. These parents told him that before the death of their children, they had experienced God as "present, just, caring, gentle, wise, in control, forgiving, and faithful" but after the death, they experienced God as "absent, unfair, unjust, unloving, cruel, vindictive, stupid, crazy, not as powerful as previously thought, unmerciful, unreliable, [and] a failure."[11]

The God whom survivors had trusted to keep them and their loved ones safe, the God whose justice they relied on to protect those who are innocent, suddenly seemed absent at best or cruel and hateful at worst. Just at the time they most needed God's care and strength, they were most overwhelmed by feelings of anger at, disappointment in, and separation from God.

This dimension of loss makes it particularly important that they receive good pastoral care. Pastoral caregivers can help them express their anger, their fear, and all their other feelings about God and to God, and relearn that God does indeed still care for them.

Psychosocial Death

As the incidence of Alzheimer's disease and other dementias increases, more and more family members will be faced with the losses and grief this form of death brings. Persons who have dementia seldom die from the disease itself. In fact, they may live with it for many years. But over time, as their brains sustain increasing damage, they will "die" to their loved ones in ways that are as hard and painful as with a physical death.

Loved ones are bereaved long before the patient actually dies. They must deal with the loss of relationship, as the person they once knew — the person they may have lived with for forty or fifty years — becomes a stranger. As dementia advances, the patient will lose her or his ability to communicate, to participate in normal life activities, and eventually to recognize even those closest to him or her.

Family members may take on more responsibilities for care and incur significant financial costs. The patient may have to give up a family home to move into an assisted-living or other care-providing community where the patient can receive more care. Good pastoral care will involve your being familiar with dementia, providing loving support for family members, and helping them connect with the resources they need.

Losses for the Pastoral Caregiver

If you are a pastoral caregiver to the dying, you must be prepared to face your own grief. Whether you are a parish pastor with long-term relationships with those who die or a chaplain who has briefer relationships, you will usually grieve when someone dies. While good pastoral care includes having good boundaries, it also includes real relationships with care-receivers. You will come to enjoy one person's positive spirit, another's sense of humor, another's stories about his former life as a railway engineer, another's courage in the face of great suffering, another's deep faith and willingness to struggle with faith questions.

Some ministry training programs encourage caregivers to develop "emotional calluses" so that caregivers are not themselves overwhelmed by all of the emotional and spiritual pain they witness. In contrast, spiritual leaders like Rabbi Schacter-Shalomi, who works extensively with end-of-life caregivers, urges that they "not allow themselves to become calloused with repeated encounters of an intense nature."[12]

Grief

Every loss, large or small, causes grief. This grief is likely to affect every dimension of the bereaved person's functioning. When a loved one is lost, that grief may be intense and last a long time. It may be manifested in healthy ways or in ways that threaten grievers' long-term well-being. Understanding what care-receivers may experience as they grieve will help you discern how best to aid them in their grief process.

Dimensions of Grief

According to D. K. Switzer, grief is "the complex interaction of affective, cognitive, physiological, and behavioral responses to the loss by any means of a person, place, thing, activity, status, bodily organ, etc., with whom (or which) a person has identified, or who (or which) has become a significant part of an individual's own-self."[13] The specific effects of grief for any individual depend on many things. Each griever — whether they are dying, a struggler, or bereaved — follows his or her own unique path. That said, the following characteristics of grief are common.

Affective (emotional) responses vary widely, although deep sadness almost always occurs. Other responses may include numbness, anxiety, fear, anger, and guilt. Grievers may feel a sense of deep loneliness or find themselves longing desperately for things to be the way they were before the loss occurred. They may feel a sense of despair, apathy, or hopelessness. Such feelings can lead to changes in grievers' social functioning, and they may avoid or withdraw from other people.

Cognitively, grievers may be confused or forgetful. Their thinking may feel slowed or foggy. This may frighten them, as they wonder whether they are "going crazy," or have had an unrecognized stroke. They may feel the loss is not real or be confused at times about what is really happening and what is imaginary. They may be disoriented, restless, or unable to focus. They may have difficulty initiating tasks or completing them. This can be particularly problematic if they are employed and have difficulty performing their work.

Physically, they may experience bodily extremes. They may feel too tired to do anything or feel overly excited, needing to do too many things. Grievers may sleep very little or may feel sleepy much of the time. They may have no appetite or be uncharacteristically hungry. They may feel physical distress, including chest pains, abdominal pains, headaches, or nausea. If these symptoms persist for very long, encourage them to check with a physician to make sure there is no organic cause for what is occurring.

Behaviorally, grievers may find themselves losing things, or forgetting to take care of basic life-tasks like meal preparation or bathing. They may experience their loved one's presence, seeing the person, hearing them, or smelling familiar smells associated with them. This can also be frightening for them, and it is reassuring for them to know this is normal. Grievers may find themselves wandering aimlessly through their home or driving without a destination in mind and having trouble finding their way home. They may tell and retell the story of their loss or refuse to talk about it at all.

Though Switzer does not describe specific *spiritual* aspects of grief, you have probably already discerned that the changes he does describe have clear spiritual implications. People may feel overwhelmed by their feelings of sadness and despair and have difficulty experiencing the hope God offers. People who cannot think clearly may have trouble noticing the ways in which God's grace does appear in their lives. People whose health is impaired may become so immersed in their physical distress that it is hard for them to attend to their spiritual healing.

Familiarity with these patterns will help you assess their level of well-being and let you reassure them that what they are experiencing is normal and will usually stop occurring over time. It will also help you discern if or when they may need a referral for someone with skills to provide services that are outside your realm of expertise.

Grief Reactions

Persons' reactions to loss depend on many factors. A particularly important one is the *nature of the loss*. Both the cause of death and age of the person who has died matter. For example, losing someone after a long battle with cancer where the person was in great pain is different from losing someone to a sudden heart attack. Losing a person to the toll taken by Alzheimer's disease over many years is different from losing someone in an auto accident. Losing a spouse or life-partner is different from losing a sibling. Losing a child to an illness is different from the loss of a child due to an accident or to suicide. And losing someone young is different from losing someone old.

The *age of the bereaved* also affects their grieving. Children and adolescents understand death differently and grieve differently from adults. That means they need special kinds of grief support. Hospice organizations offer special workshops for children, teens, and their families, which can be invaluable for those in your care. Older people who have more life experience will grieve differently, both because they may have more coping skills as a result of their maturity, and because of their different relationship with the one who has died.

Perhaps the most important factor affecting the grief process is the *survivor's mental and spiritual health and capacity*. Persons who are ordinarily mentally healthy usually manage grief far better than those struggling before their loss with depression, bipolar disorder, or another major mental illness. People who have strong faith or other communities to support them spiritually also tend to engage in the grief process in healthier ways. As is true in other forms of pastoral care, helping connect those who are grieving with appropriate support groups is one of the most vital things you can do as a caregiver.

Complicated Grief

While every grief experience is individual and unique and there is no "right way" to grieve, it is important to know that usually, over time, people do move through the grief process to a place of resolution and healing. It may take months or years, but if people attend to and work with their grief they eventually move to a new place of restoration and well-being.

Sometimes, for reasons that are not always clear, this movement does not happen. When individuals refuse to grieve or get bound up in the grieving process, they may become "stuck" emotionally, cognitively, spiritually, or behaviorally in ways that are unhealthy and can even be life-threatening. When a person becomes stuck in this way, it is referred to as complicated, delayed, or morbid grief.

A signal that this may be happening is when a person who has experienced a loss denies it has happened. For example, a young adult who has been turned down by the college of her choice might say, "I know they're going to change their minds and let me in after all," or an adult who has lost a cherished job might say, "They're going to realize they were wrong in letting me go and call and offer me my job back." In the case of bereavement, signals that this may be happening include the griever's continuing reference to the deceased person in the present tense (confusion about this right after the death is normal), declining to hold a memorial service or funeral (although culturally this is becoming more common overall), or refusing to visit the cemetery after the interment.

It may become clear that some in your care are in the same place with their grieving six months or a year after the loss as they were immediately after it occurred. You (or a family member or friend) may notice that a griever stays focused on his or her sadness, anger, or depression without moving toward peaceful resolution. If you believe a bereaved person may be experiencing complicated grief, check in and follow up. This kind of grief can lead to clinical anxiety, major depression, or suicide, all outcomes which are usually preventable with appropriate care.

Unrecognized Grief

In recent years, researchers have begun to explore what is called unrecognized, unsanctioned, or disenfranchised grief. This refers to grief that has been viewed in the past as not "legitimate," and therefore grievers have not been offered pastoral (or social) support or care in their suffering.

Gay and lesbian couples, partners or family members of those who have died from AIDS, life-partners who are heterosexual but unmarried, those who lose pre-term babies, and birth parents who have relinquished their infants have often been denied the right to grieve their losses. In addition, the deep grief experienced from traumatic losses like incest, rape, or other assault, the loss of meaningful work at retirement, the loss of a partner or spouse through divorce or to a dementing illness, may be unrecognized or unmarked. Even the loss of a pet can be profound for the bereaved, yet is often minimized.

Persons suffering from these losses grieve just as deeply as those who suffer other, widely recognized kinds of loss and need just as much pastoral care. A deep need in our faith communities is to develop more helpful practices to acknowledge and validate many kinds of loss and to help survivors move to new places of wholeness and healing.

Your Grief

Some suggest that the grief experienced by caregivers is also unsanctioned. Because it is "your job" to care for others, many people are surprised to learn that you too grieve at the loss of someone in your care. However, if you are in full relationship with those you serve, when they die, you will hurt. And if you minister in a setting that involves long relationships with others, your grief may be deep and long-lasting.

Yet, in the role of caring for the family, members of the congregation, and others, you must sometimes postpone your grieving. If you work in a ministry setting where deaths are frequent, you may find your grief accumulating if you don't stop and take time to experience it and process it.

It will be helpful for you to have a support group. While few communities offer Grief Groups for Pastors, a clergy supervision group can serve that function. A spiritual director may also be able to help you mourn and heal. And you will need to develop spiritual practices to maintain and nurture your own faith and spiritual well-being, which we will consider further in chapter 4.

Chapter Three

Theological Issues and End-of-Life Care

We do not live to ourselves, and we do not die to ourselves. If we live, we live to the Lord, and if we die, we die to the Lord; so then, whether we live or whether we die, we are the Lord's. For to this end Christ died and lived again, so that he might be Lord of both the dead and the living. — Romans 14:7–9

We Are the Lord's

The call came at 1:00 a.m. The pastor was sound asleep, and groped for the telephone in the dark. The person on the other end introduced herself, explaining she was the sister of a woman who, with her husband, belonged to the pastor's church. There had been a bad accident, she said, and she and the rest of the family were at the E.R. of the local hospital. Could the pastor please come?

She dressed quickly and was at the hospital twenty minutes later. She could see the shock and fear on the faces of her parishioners and the extended family members who had gathered with them. No medical personnel had talked to them since they had arrived at the hospital, when they were told that their son had been in a serious rollover accident, and was badly hurt. As they sat together and talked, the mother kept asking, "Why? Why would God let this happen?" The father, clearly furious, yelled, "God is just trying to get him to clean up his act. You know he drinks too much. Well, this is God teaching him a lesson!"

Pastoral Listening as a Theological Act

As noted in chapter 1, pastoral caregivers bring a particular per-spective to each caregiving encounter — one grounded in both the care-receiver's and the caregiver's relationship with God. Pastoral caregivers come as visible representatives of the Invisible One in whom we live and move and have our being. They also come within the context of a community that explicitly understands itself to be part of God's people and the body of Christ.

Pastoral encounters and conversations always involve an awareness that there are three partners in the situation: the care-receiver, the caregiver, and the God who holds and cares for them both. So both care-receivers and caregivers intentionally invite God into the space and into the discussion, listening together for what God might have to say and do in whatever is happening, what one author calls "Godward listening."[14]

This awareness alone is not enough to offer effective care. You must also be able to articulate what it is you believe about God and God's activity in the world, and why you believe those things. More important, you must learn to help others articulate what they believe and why. In ministerial terms, you must be aware of your own theology and that of the care-receiver.

The word "theology" comes from two roots: *theos*, which means "God," and *logos*, which means "word" or "understanding." So theology is "a way of organizing our thinking about God"[15] and the words we use to express that organization and understanding. Our theology is our "words about God."

For example, some people view God as a loving, compassionate being. Others view God as a judging, punitive being. Some believe that God is intimately involved with every single thing that happens in the world. Others believe that God is more distant, caring perhaps about what happens, but not intervening directly in persons' lives. Some understand God as an impersonal creative principle. Whatever a person believes about God and about God's interaction with humankind and the world, he will usually feel quite strongly about those beliefs, and she will usually feel she has very good reasons to believe what she does.

Pastoral caregivers help others reflect theologically. They help care-receivers become clearer about their own faith understandings. They may or may not, depending on their particular tradition, share their own theological views.

As they help those who are struggling name their deepest questions and speak about and with God, those care-receivers are likely to experience new clarity, comfort, and hope. This is conversational territory that most other caregivers are uncomfortable entering. Your willingness to explore these deep meanings with those who are hurting will mean more than you can know and can lead to deep healing for those who are suffering.

Key Theological Concerns

When people are healthy and life is going well, questions about who and what God is like and how God is or isn't involved in the events of daily life may be interesting, challenging, and worth some reflection and prayer. When they or someone they love is near death, such questions become much more imperative and no longer simply interesting.

Care-receivers dealing with end-of-life situations may have many questions about God and God's activity as they struggle to find meaning, hope, and connection in their circumstances. Here we will consider some questions that are particularly likely to arise in these settings.

Meaning

People of all ages are meaning-makers. We want our lives to have purpose and significance — and our deaths as well. We want it to matter that we have lived. We may also want it to matter how we die. From children to elders, everyone who is dying grapples with these needs.

When someone is dying, they and their loved ones are likely to ask, Why? Why me, God? God, how could you let this happen?

He's such a good man — he doesn't deserve this. She has three small children, and they need their mother! Lord, how could you do this to her? To him? To me? Why?

The theological term for these kinds of questions is "theodicy." The word comes from two roots that mean "God" and "justice." The problem of theodicy is this: If God is God — which for most people includes the belief that God is good and loving, and for many people the belief that God is omnipotent (all-powerful), why and how do bad things — "unjust" things like cancer and miscarriages and murders — happen? Why do bad things happen to good people, or to anyone? If God is good and loving, why does God let those things happen?

Theologians have wrestled with these questions for centuries. The Bible simply does not provide clear answers. It says, for example, "that all things work together for good for those who love God" (Rom. 8:28). But what about all the biblical accounts of genocides, murders, infant deaths, and more? And what about today's evening news stories of genocides, murders, infant deaths, and more? Most faithful people want to believe that God is all-good and all-loving and all-powerful, but how do they square that with all the terrible things that happen in the world and in their lives, day after day?

It is the very question that the parents in the E.R. story are asking. Why would God let their son be in a terrible accident? The father's answer, interestingly, reflects some trust that God's purposes are positive (to teach the son a lesson he needs to learn), even if the method (the accident) is not.

Historically, because of the lack of clear scriptural guidance, theologians have turned to other sources — to popular philosophy, the sciences, other faith perspectives — to try to resolve this conundrum. And they have arrived at many different answers. Space does not permit us to cover those here, but it would benefit you and your care-receivers to read more about this in the recommended resources in the Appendix.

There are as yet no perfectly clear answers to why suffering and evil exist. That means as a pastoral caregiver, you must become comfortable with uncertainty — both yours and that of your care-receivers — about this most central issue.

Hope

Not surprisingly, when people are struggling with pain, fear, uncertainty, they also have a profound need for hope. They ask, "Why not just give up?" "How can I keep enduring this?" "Why should I keep on going?" "Will things ever get any better?"

For people of faith, one dimension of hope has to do with "eschatology." "Escha" refers to "last" or "final," and you have already learned that "ology" refers to "our words about." So eschatology has to do with our words about the last or final things. About what happens after this life is over, and what happens in the future.

Over the centuries, theologians have wondered about the existence of the soul and what happens to it when earthly life is finished. They have debated and argued about the existence and nature of heaven and hell. They have wrestled with the meaning of resurrection for human beings as promised through Christ's resurrection. And they have speculated about what will happen to the dead on the Last Day.

Again, the Bible does not offer clear answers. Ideas about heaven appear in both Testaments, and includes the view that heaven is where God resides with the angels and God's saints, and, in the New Testament, with Jesus Christ. It is also the place where righteous people dwell forever after their deaths.

The concept of hell has a more complicated history. Its meaning changes from the Old Testament to the New Testament. Over time, in most Christian thought, hell has come to refer to the idea of eternal suffering and punishment for a person's wrongdoings while on earth. Far worse, this eternal death involves separation forever from others and from God.

As is the case with theodicy, these conclusions about the afterlife lead to a theological problem. Christians affirm the all-encompassing love of God, from which nothing can separate anyone. How, then, could this loving God condemn some people to an eternity of suffering? Ultimately, shouldn't salvation prevail?

While your care-receivers may not be interested in these debates, they will want to know "what comes next." "Where will my husband go after he dies?" "I haven't always been a good person; am I going to hell?" "Is my stillborn baby in heaven?" They may well find hope in the affirmation that in the next life one is at peace and no longer suffers.

They will also need sources of daily hope while they are still in this life. That may mean hope for a cure for their (or their loved one's) disease, or it may take other forms. For example, imagine a fifty-year-old teacher diagnosed with prostate cancer. He might first hope to be able to finish teaching the school term. Next he may hope to be released from the hospital to celebrate Christmas with his family. Finally he may hope that his death will be pain-free and peaceful. Each hope a person has is important to acknowledge and bless.

You will offer hope by your very presence, reminding those who are hurting that somehow, through you, God is also present with them. You may also be able to offer hope through the prayers and rituals you offer or through shared Scripture. And in the conversations the two of you share with God, you may encourage the care-receiver to consider ways God has strengthened and supported her or him in the past, with an eye and heart to how that might be possible in the present and future.

Connection

Connection or "community" is both a theological and a practical dimension of care. One of the most important new understandings in the field of pastoral care is that persons both give and receive care in communal contexts.[16]

As described in chapter 1, you as caregiver are embedded in many communities, as are care-receivers. As a pastoral caregiver, you represent the wider faith community. In addition, you have also been shaped by your particular racial, ethnic, socioeconomic, and other communities. This is also true for care-receivers, who embody their own set of community-based particularities. Both your and their specific communities shape how care is offered and received.

For people who are dying and for their loved ones, community is a central need. They need to know they are not alone, that there are people around them who care for them, and that they are part of God's beloved community.

An important theological issue that may arise in this area is reconciliation. Most people have impaired relationships with others in their lives, and dying people may need to be reconciled with those with whom they are in conflict or from whom they are estranged. The dying father may ask, "What shall I do about Karen, my daughter who I haven't spoken to for years?" Or the adult daughter may wonder, "What can I do to find some peace about my Dad? He's dying, and I still hate him for abusing me when I was a kid."

People who know their lives will end soon are often concerned about unfinished business, including broken or damaged relationships from their past. Reconciling with people from whom one has become estranged can bring a deeply important sense of closure and peace, both for the person who is dying and for those in relationship with her or him.

The Bible speaks much more clearly to this issue than to the two previous topics. At the Creation, God gives *adam*, the earth creature, a companion because "it is not good for [human beings] to be alone" (Gen. 2:18). Both the Old and New Testaments are filled with stories focused on families, relationships, and covenants. It is clear that people are created as relational beings and that we must have connection with others or we die — physically, emotionally, and spiritually.

Those who are dying seem to have a deep awareness of this truth. They do not simply want but need to heal broken relationships and reconnect with those most important to them. In fact, the need for reconciliation can be so intense that it can forestall death itself. Professional caregivers can relate many stories in which a person lingered on, barely alive, until a significant other person arrived, and healing words could be spoken.

Supportive care, when dying persons are conscious, involves helping them realistically examine their own role and responsibility when conflict or difficulty happened, and the role and responsibility of the other. It also involves encouraging them to reflect on their understandings of both human and divine forgiveness and how that is extended to them and to others. Caregivers who can facilitate connection and reconciliation offer care-receivers a profound gift.

Helping Care-Receivers

A longstanding theological task of pastoral caregivers is guidance. Historically, that has often meant telling care-receivers which theological beliefs are "correct" and which are not, and how those beliefs should direct their choices and actions (including those involved in end-of-life situations). In many faith communities today, this task has more to do with encouraging care-receivers to do their own theological reflection, aided by the pastor. This means helping them name and struggle with theological issues that arise for them, assisted and guided by their particular faith tradition, and by the Holy Spirit.

Your Theology

In chapter 1, you were encouraged to reflect on your own experiences with death and dying and your thoughts and feelings about this area of life and of pastoral care. As in every arena of caregiving, your theology will shape those thoughts and feelings. So it is important to be aware of what you believe and why you hold those particular beliefs. It is also helpful to be aware that your beliefs may be challenged, even changed in light of what you learn in each caregiving situation.

When faced with great suffering, the ready answers of faith you once had may suddenly seem inadequate. Why would a loving God allow a just-married couple to be killed by a drunken driver on their honeymoon getaway? What kind of comfort can God offer to the young man who has been a deacon and a choir member, has surgery for testicular cancer, and learns he will never biologically father children? Where is God for the wife of fifty-eight years, in tremendous pain from uterine cancer, whose husband has abandoned her because he "can't stand to see her suffer that way"? What does your faith tradition say? What does your experience say? What is God saying, right now?

While you don't need to have the "right" words or the "right" answers to questions like these — because, as we have seen, there may be none — you do need to have given them some thought and prayer and be willing to continue to wrestle with them. Only then will you be able to help others in their struggles to integrate their faith beliefs with their experiences and to help them find the grounded, realistic, and meaningful hope that faith offers.

Further, just as you will encourage care-receivers to attend to their relationships with God, you will need to attend to and nurture yours as well. Develop spiritual practices that will deepen, nurture, and sustain your relationship with the Holy. For some of you that will mean a deeper prayer discipline; for others it may mean exploring new forms of prayer. For still others it may mean finding a spiritual director, or trying new ways of being in relationship with God, like the ancient practices of *lectio divina* or walking a sacred labyrinth, or contemporary practices like journaling or spiritual dancing. The Appendix contains resources to explore.

Listening Skills

In addition to a willingness to reflect theologically with care-receivers, helpful listening involves a set of skills and forms of awareness that you may have acquired elsewhere, especially if you have a counseling background. You will need to know how to offer a pastoral presence, to manage your own anxiety, to create a sense of safety for the care-receiver, to attend to both verbal and nonverbal information and to ask the kinds of questions that will help the conversation go to deeper levels. If these are new skills for you, the resources in the Appendix offer excellent instruction.

Two important skills will support fruitful caregiving. One is the art of learning to really listen to care-receivers, to spend considerably more of your time listening than speaking, and to listen with them to and for God. The second is the art of learning when and how to use questions to help them reflect more deeply. As a general rule, open-ended questions, such as "So tell me what you think God is like," or "Where do you see God in what is happening right now?" are much more helpful in facilitating reflection than closed-ended questions such as "Do you believe that God is loving?" or "Do you think God is with you in this?"

Spiritual Needs Assessment

Spiritual assessment is something pastors have always done, although not always consciously. Briefly, it means using well-developed listening skills to discern where the care-receiver is spiritually, and what her or his key spiritual needs are at the present time. Does she need reassurance that she will survive the loss of her life-companion? Does he need hope about the future of his children as he sees his life coming quickly to a close? Where does she see God in what is happening? What does he most need from God in what he is going through?

There are many approaches to spiritual assessment, from very informal conversations to highly structured interviews. While you will develop your own practice for assessment with experience, you are encouraged to begin your work grounded in a model that has already been tested and found effective, like one of those in the recommended resources.

Sensitive Responses

Talking about God is challenging, particularly for people new to ministry. You may feel embarrassed, uncomfortable, or awkward. You may still be developing your own theological vocabulary and your ability to listen and respond effectively. You may wonder if you're doing it "right," given that your awareness of the way in which caregivers speak of and listen for the Holy matters deeply, especially when care-receivers are greatly distressed.

It is important to speak care-fully about God. Speaking that is full of care does not assume that the care-receiver shares your faith understandings, nor that your words about God are necessarily correct. It does embrace the wide variety of images and understandings of God found in the Scriptures and throughout history in the church. And it accepts that those images and understandings have changed over several millennia and are still changing.

Listening about and for God is also challenging. When care-receivers raise hard theological questions, most caregivers' first response is to offer them answers. "No, Don, God didn't give you this disease." "Perhaps, Karen, God is trying to show others what real grace looks like in the way you are dealing with your dying." "Well, Ken, let me tell you what the Bible says about the importance of reconciliation."

When that happens to you, please restrain yourself. Often caregivers' need to say something immediately comes from their own anxiety combined with their fervent desire to help the other person. Until you have spent some time listening carefully to the person and her or his story, you will have no idea what answers she is seeking, or what he most needs to hear from God. Only after you and the care-receiver have developed some relationship together in the presence of God will the two of you be able to hear the answers God is offering.

Sometimes what others most need is not your words, but silence. For example, imagine that a patient's husband tells you his wife has just been diagnosed with Stage IV breast cancer, or a parishioner tells you her husband has just been moved to a nursing home, where he will live out his last days. There may be little or nothing meaningful that you can say, except "I'm so sorry." While you might feel you ought to say more, silence or a brief but sincere response may be what is most helpful.

When you are with a person who is greatly distressed, it can be difficult both to remain silent and feel connected. Yet simply sitting with another, sharing your calm and compassionate presence, knowing that you both are held in God's care, can be immensely healing. Caregivers do well to learn to respect the silence in which God's voice may be heard more clearly than it can be in the midst of noise.

When it is time to talk, you need to become clear about what the caregiver wants or needs from your visit and your conversation, and from God. Where are they experiencing God (if they are) in what is presently happening? How might you help them deepen that experience?

Sometimes you will find that a care-receiver's theology is very different from yours. For example, a care-receiver may suggest that something bad has happened because God is punishing him. You may believe that God does not intentionally cause bad things to happen to people.

When this happens, it may be tempting to contradict or correct the other person's "mistaken" beliefs. In most faith traditions, however, that is not the pastoral caregiver's job. And in situations of great anguish — as is the case in many end-of-life settings — it is especially unhelpful to suggest that the care-receivers are wrong, or that you know more about God, or about their relationship with God, than they do. Instead, your primary task is to remain in genuine relationship with them, engaging them as you are able in reflecting on their beliefs.

This does not mean you must agree with beliefs that contradict yours or feel compelled to make theological statements that violate your own pastoral integrity. In most settings you can offer a neutral response, such as "when things like this happen, I wonder why, too," rather than explicitly agreeing or disagreeing with them. If they belong to a faith community, you may also want to offer to help them contact their own pastor to provide support that will be consonant with their beliefs and theological needs. Finally, you can simply support them with your compassionate presence and your prayers.

Culture Matters

Persons' experiences, interpretations, and understandings of every-thing — including end-of-life experiences — are profoundly shaped by their culture. This includes cultures in which they were raised (e.g., their family of rearing, their ethnic affiliation, their faith community) and those communities in which they presently live (e.g., their current family, ethnic affiliations, pri-mary social communities, faith community if any, and the popular culture that surrounds them).

The way in which care is received — and is offered — is shaped by both the care-receiver's and the caregiver's cultural back-grounds and identities.[17] Consider this example. Steve is a hospice chaplain. He is Euro-American, in his early thirties, ordained in the United Methodist tradition. One afternoon he is paged to the chronic-care unit, to see the family of a Mr. Hernandez, who has just died. He is told that the hospital had attempted to reach a Roman Catholic priest because that was the patient's religious faith, but no priest was available.

When he enters the patient's room, he finds a dozen fam-ily members, mostly women in their mid-to-late-seventies, all Hispanic. A woman is lying on the bed holding the body of Mr. Hernandez and sobbing loudly. Steve guesses from her appar-ent age, roughly the same as Mr. Hernandez, that she is the grieving new widow. When he introduces himself as the hospi-tal chaplain, the women begin weeping even louder, several of them screaming out with grief. The noise and great emotional expressiveness jar him as he mentally contrasts it with the quieter grief he has experienced from most Euro-Americans. He becomes anxious, and wonders how he will minister to these hurting people who seem so different from himself.

Because culture plays such an important role in the sharing of care, it is well for caregivers to be aware of their own cultural identity and assumptions, as well as to know as much as they can about the culture of those to whom they offer care. Some of the resources in the Appendix will help you learn more about pastoral care with persons from cultures different from your own.

It is also helpful to be aware of popular culture. Watch movies like Wit and The Bucket List. Read novels like The Shack and The Art of Racing in the Rain, and nonfiction popular works like When Bad Things Happen to Good People and The Last Lecture. Notice what theological truths they affirm and what questions they raise. Consider how they influence the theology of those for whom you care. Their theological messages may be as significant to care-receivers as those encountered in their faith communities. You do well to understand as much as you can how all those things influences persons' "words about God."

Pastoral Theology as an Act of Growth

Not only does your theology shape your care, but what happens in your caregiving will also shape your theology. As you listen to others' life-stories and faith understandings, as you enter together into some of the most painful and powerful and sacred moments of persons' lives, as you are truly engaged in the work you are doing, your understanding of who God is and how God works will be transformed.

This "action-reflection model" means that you will offer an act of pastoral care, pay attention to what happens, and both thoughtfully and prayerfully reflect on the experience afterward. That reflection may include a strengthening of your existing theological beliefs, it may challenge them, and sometimes it leads to a reconsideration of them. Your resulting understandings will then shape the next pastoral encounter you have, and the next, and the next.

Chapter Four

Faith Resources:
The Pastoral Caregiver's Tool Kit

Even though I walk through the darkest valley,
I fear no evil; for you are with me;
your rod and your staff — they comfort me.
                                            — Psalm 23:4

You Comfort Me?

Eva was a middle-aged African American woman scheduled for surgery to determine whether she had cancer. She arrived at the hospital shortly before dawn, was checked in and prepped for the surgery. Frightened both because this was her first experience of surgery and because of the seriousness of her condition, she was relieved when a woman wearing a cross and a chaplain's badge walked into her pre-op cubicle.

The chaplain briefly introduced herself and offered to pray for Eva. She accepted gratefully and closed her eyes, expecting to be soothed and comforted. Moments later, her eyes snapped open as the chaplain prayed, "Father, heal him with this surgery, and comfort him in his distress" — then abruptly stopped, realizing what she had said.

It was clear to Eva that this was a prayer routinely used before surgeries, apparently for male patients, and that the chaplain had simply repeated it, paying no attention either to Eva's personhood, or to the prayer-language. It was devastating for Eva, who felt discounted and disappointed — a far cry from the reassurance and comfort she had hoped for.

One's Faith Tradition

If you are providing pastoral care, you are affiliated with a faith tradition. In chapter 3, as you read about theological issues, you may have found yourself nodding in some places and shaking your head in others. While this book tries to present a "general Christian" overview of faith beliefs and practices, there are many differences between various Christian traditions, just as there are many differences between Christian and non-Christian traditions.

In the story above, the caregiver came from a tradition different from that of the care-receiver. In the chaplain's tradition, pastoral care is primarily liturgical-sacramental in nature. Prayer-language is formal and usually uses male pronouns, assuming they refer to all persons. Theologically she assumes God works in a certain way. In Eva's tradition, pastoral care is primarily relational in nature, and understandings of God's activity are somewhat different. Prayer-language is more informal and gender-inclusive. It isn't surprising that Eva found the prayer discordant and distressing.

Clearly, this is not what you want to have happen in your caregiving. Awareness of both your faith tradition and that of care-receivers will help prevent it from happening.

People's traditions also shape how they perceive the role of the pastor and which faith resources are helpful in times of difficulty. For example, faith backgrounds affect whether and how a caregiver prays with others and how that prayer is received. Traditions affect how helpful Scripture readings may be to those who are troubled and how and when caregivers share Scripture with others. Finally, traditions determine people's understanding of the sacraments and their role in pastoral care, as well as of the appropriateness of using other faith rituals in offering care.

If you are caring mostly for people from your own tradition, they are likely to share many of your understandings about these things. Even then, you may sometimes be surprised. For example, a person for whom you assumed the twenty-third Psalm would be comforting may respond to it with distress instead, or someone to whom you offer Communion may refuse to partake. Try not to make assumptions about others' receptivity to faith resources, even when you think you know them well. Instead, learn to listen carefully for their "words about God" and about which faith resources will truly encourage and sustain them.

If you work in a chaplaincy setting, you may offer care to many people whose faith traditions are different from yours and who therefore may have different perceptions about various faith resources. It is helpful to know something about other traditions, so you can engage such care-receivers in fruitful ways. In any situation, the most important thing is for you to listen and learn from them which resources will be most supportive.

Prayer

This chapter considers five major "tools" in your pastoral tool-kit. The first three, prayer, Scripture, and the sacraments, are common to nearly all Christian traditions. The fourth, additional healing rituals, is more commonly used in traditions that embrace a wider range of ways for connecting persons with the healing power of the Holy. The fifth, yourself, is the most important "tool" of all, although one that caregivers sometimes forget.

We begin with prayer, because almost all faith traditions embrace prayer as an essential practice for connecting with the Holy. So it is the one faith resource most care-receivers will actively seek, be open to, and find comforting.

Your Prayer-Practice

Before you can pray helpfully with and for others, you must first have a prayer-practice of your own. Your practice is what grounds you in and nurtures your relationship with God. And that relationship is the place from which you offer care to others.

Your prayer-practice may take many different forms. Some people prefer to pray when they are alone, perhaps with the use of prayer-beads. Others find it more nourishing to be part of a prayer-community. Some pray by reflecting on Scripture, others through centering prayer, others by spiritual journaling, and still others by meditative walking. Explore a range of prayer-practices, and find those forms that engage you and nourish your relationship with God.

Praying Out Loud

Many ministers fear praying "out loud." While they may have rich and nourishing personal prayer-lives, the thought of praying with or for others in a public space may make them feel awkward or self-conscious. These concerns may be heightened in situations where the emotional and spiritual stakes seem high, as they often are in end-of-life settings.

A friend shared a story about her early days of chaplaincy. She was called to the bedside of a retired Episcopal priest (she was ordained in another denomination). He was very ill, possibly dying, and asked her to pray for him. She felt sick with anxiety. She was afraid of not sounding "holy" enough in her prayer-language, of not saying it "right," of "sounding silly." She was afraid of what the patient and the attending medical staff would think about the "quality" of her prayer.

You may recognize some of those feelings. Praying with others may make you too feel uncomfortable, inadequate, or exposed. If so, you will be glad to learn that with time and experience, those feelings tend to diminish.

Yes, praying with and for others is an awesome responsibility. They are relying on you to convey their deepest concerns and needs to God, often when they are unable to do that themselves. It is a most sacred trust.

The good news is you do know how to pray. Most of you have been doing it all your lives. Long before you had any formal theological vocabulary, your five-year-old self saw God in the flowers, felt God in your puppy's warm licking, heard God in your mother's bedtime story, and felt God in your dad's hug when you fell out of a tree and hurt yourself. Your heart has always known how to say "thank you" and "please." The challenge for you now is to learn how to listen carefully for others' heart-knowings and translate them into words or images or gestures that help connect them and you and the Holy One.

Shaping Prayers

The dying, or their family, will often want you to pray for them. Even when the person is unconscious, those around her may find solace in prayer. As in all situations where you pray for others, it is important to focus on what they want and need from the prayer.

There is no right or wrong way to pray. Yet as our pre-surgery prayer story shows, there are more and less helpful ways to pray with care-receivers.

The language you use matters, though not in the way you may think. The concern is not about choosing words that sound "holy enough," or knowing when to use "Thee" and "Thy." It is about using language that is sensitive to care-receivers' concerns and theologies (which, as noted, may be different from yours).

To do that, before you pray, you must listen. What are his deepest concerns and fears? What is she most hoping for? How does he perceive God? What would help her feel that God cares about her? And what does he need from you and from the prayer you can offer on his behalf?

You must also know whether or not the person wishes to be prayed for. Unless the person is unconscious, you should simply ask. Questions like "Would you like me to pray for you?" or "would it be okay if I pray for you?" empower them and clarify some of their pastoral needs.

If they do want prayer, even if you have listened carefully and believe you know what they want and need, it is good practice to check. It may feel awkward at first, but you can ask directly, "What would you like me to pray for?" You may be surprised when the woman who has been talking for an hour about her fears of a future without her dying husband asks you to pray that she can find a home for his dog. Or when the man who has been focused on his worries about his partner's future asks you to pray for their son instead.

Listen. Ask. Pray their request, if you can do so with theological integrity. When dying persons are not able to express their desires, you may wish to pray that they experience peace rather than fear, or express gratitude for their life, or reassurance that their loved ones will be all right after they are gone.

If you are uncomfortable praying spontaneously, and many new caregivers are, you have other options. Most faith communities have books of worship that include suitable prayers for end-of-life situations. Or prepare simple prayers (for reassurance, comfort, hope, or other likely needs) before visiting, then modify them as needed once you are in the situation and have listened to the care-receiver.

Scripture

The Scriptures offer countless stories about healing and curing. In the Hebrew Bible, when the widow of Zarephath, near death, meets Elijah, we see that God can provide even in the face of impossibility. As King David suffers through his infant son's illness and death, we see that recovery from loss is possible. Many of the Psalms and the book of Lamentations echo the cries of those for whom you care. They articulate feelings of anger, despair, loss, and protest against the most painful parts of life and lift those feelings to God. These stories validate the reality of care-receivers' present-day anguish and point toward the ever-present care of God and hope for the future.

In the New Testament we find parents losing beloved children, sisters losing brothers, people suffering themselves from life-threatening illnesses. When Martha and Mary lose their brother, Lazarus, Jesus joins them, and we learn that when we are weeping, God weeps with us. When Jesus raises the widow of Nain's dead son, we see that God sends help when we are in the midst of distress, and that miracles are possible. In the story of the hemorrhaging woman, we learn not to give up, no matter how hopeless things seem. These passages, and many others, can be powerful tools in caregiving.

Scriptural Knowledge

To effectively use a resource you must know it well. You may already feel knowledgable about the Bible, its origins, and different modes of interpretation, and you may be comfortable sharing Scripture with others. Or you may not. If you have spent little time with the Bible, you may need to learn more to use it effectively in caregiving.

Along with a personal prayer-practice, it is useful to develop a regular Bible study practice. If you are serving in a parish and preaching regularly, this will become part of your weekly routine. If you serve in a different ministry setting, you may need to develop a study discipline.

Even if you have read the Bible all your life, there is always more to learn — especially when using Scripture in a new way, like as a tool for healing. Find a good commentary and combine this reading with regular immersion in the biblical texts themselves. Think about passages and stories that have been helpful to you when you were hurting and so might be helpful to others. Find or create a colleague group to meet regularly, and seriously explore the Scriptures. Read the text — pray the text — consider the text through the lenses of scholars, pastoral caregivers, and care-receivers. The better grasp you have of the texts at both intellectual and emotional levels, the more effectively you will be able to use Scripture in your ministry.

The Power of Story

Scripture is such a powerful tool for learning, growth, and healing because it is first and foremost about story. While many people can quote the Ten Commandments or a favorite Psalm, the biblical texts most likely to have touched people deeply are the stories. An invitation to "tell me something you like in the Bible" is likely to elicit a hero story like that of King David or Queen Esther, a pilgrimage story like that of Moses or Ruth, or one of the many stories about Jesus.

Since the dawn of humanity, stories have told people who they are and how they fit into their community and the world. They offer compelling images of what has been and what can be, grounding listeners in their shared past and leading them into an imagined future. From a caregiving perspective, stories help care-receivers make sense of their experiences, offer them new perspectives, and connect caregivers and care-receivers with each other, with the larger community past and present, and with God.

Stories and Pastoral Care

As you listen to a care-receiver, his personal story may remind you of a favorite story of your own from Scripture. Resist the temptation, however, to share it immediately. Instead, keep listening. It will be more helpful to him to discover his own relevant healing stories than to listen to yours.

How do you help caregivers discover that? Listen for those things that are important to them about their past and their present. What was their family of origin like, and how did they fit into it? What is their current family configuration? With whom do they have positive relationships, and with whom do they have negative ones? How have those relationships changed over time? What emotional themes seem to resonate — joy, despair, abundance, lack, freedom, restriction?

What are their images of God? Where do those images come from? What has their relationship with God been like in the past, and what is it like now? How do they nurture that relationship? Where do they feel God has fallen short for them? Where has God provided?

Listen with both the ears of your heart and of your mind. What biblical stories, if any, are most significant to care-receivers' faith understandings? If they offer an example, explore the meaning that story, passage, or biblical character has for them. How does she see the example as related to her present situation and concerns? How is the story or character meaningful to him in understanding his own life? What other stories or passages might help them expand their understanding of God and God's activity in transformative and healing ways?

Some caregivers may have trouble thinking of a biblical story that resonates for them in their present situation. But if they seem interested in trying this approach for healing, you may offer a story of your own as a way of helping them into the biblical world and as a model for how stories might help them.

Some care-receivers will find great comfort from you simply reading the Bible to them. Your ability to find "that thing about 'for everything there is a season'" or "the thing about God being our shepherd" will be a real gift for them. On the other hand, some care-receivers will find your reading to them or encouraging them to read the Bible themselves uncomfortable or distancing. Careful listening will help you discern what seems true for an individual, and you can proceed accordingly.

The Sacraments

In the early history of the Christian church, pastoral care was offered by community members to one another. Following the model that Jesus and the early Christian community established, caring for one another was simply part of practicing one's faith. Later, as the church became more institutionalized, rules were changed, and only specially authorized people (priests and other recognized ministers) were allowed to provide such care. The understanding of pastoral care shifted from holistic healing that encompassed body, mind, and spirit to a theological equation of healing with salvation, in which ritual became increasingly important in offering care.

A "sacrament" is a special form of faith ritual. It is usually understood as a practice that Jesus himself initiated or participated in. So in most Protestant traditions, two sacraments, baptism and Holy Communion, are recognized. In the Roman Catholic tradition and other faiths, additional sacraments are recognized.

Sacraments usually include both sacred words and special actions. They may also involve elements of water, bread and wine or juice, oil, fire, and incense. These elements are usually given by the celebrant (the minister, priest, or other authorized minister) to those receiving the sacrament.

Although occasionally persons nearing the end of their lives may wish to be baptized, it is the sacrament of Holy Communion that is more likely to be shared in end-of-life settings. It may be deeply meaningful to those who are very ill or who are grieving, because it reminds them of their connection both to Jesus Christ and to the wider church. Because of its physicality, it can provide a kind of comfort that words alone cannot. For members of some traditions, the sacrament of reconciliation can also be very powerful for those who are dying or about to lose a loved one to death.

You are already familiar with the sacraments recognized in your tradition and know when and how they are typically used in worship. You may need to learn when and how they are used in pastoral caregiving.

For example, Holy Communion (the Eucharist) is typically shared with elements of bread and juice or wine. If the recipient is seriously ill or dying, however, they may be unable to swallow well. Or if they are facing surgery and are NPO (not allowed anything by mouth), they may need to receive the sacrament in a different way. You may be able to share the juice on a moistened swab, or you may simply read the liturgy and use expressive gestures (e.g., touching the bread to their lips without their actually ingesting it) instead. Be sure to check with medical staff before sharing Communion in these circumstances so you do not endanger the person who is ill.

If you will be giving care to persons from other faith traditions, it will serve you well to become familiar with their sacramental understandings and practices too. Reading, study, and conversations with pastoral colleagues can all help you with this learning.

Healing Rituals

Sometimes traditional faith resources will be inadequate or unhelpful to meet the spiritual needs of dying or bereaved people. For example, only recently have some denominations added to their books of worship prayers for the loss of a child before birth. For many situations you will encounter there are no suggested prayers in denominational resources. And for some care-receivers, prayers or Scripture or the sacraments may not be especially meaningful.

So it is well for caregivers to be able to create rituals that will be meaningful, if that is permitted in your faith tradition and in the care-receiver's. You can use symbols like water, oil, stones, fire, and flowers, which have had deep spiritual significance since ancient times. Water symbolizes cleansing, renewal, and healing. Oil is a sign of anointing or blessing. Stones connect us with the earth and with the Ground of Our Being. Fire and light symbolize the presence of the Divine. Flowers symbolize beauty and God's goodness. Adding a few healing words — perhaps a Scripture passage, a familiar prayer, or a favorite poem — to the sharing of one of these symbols can touch care-receivers in deep, healing ways.

Created rituals can be very simple. For example, inviting a bereaved person to write a letter to the person who has died expressing important things that were left unsaid before the death, then burning the letter, symbolically lifts that person's thoughts and feelings to God and helps release some of their pain. Or piling stones in an intentional way in a place that was important to the deceased can serve as a memorial and release some physical and emotional energy for the griever.

Rituals can also be complex, involving several people, symbols, and actions. Gathering other loved ones into the ritual provides a visual symbol of community, and the energy shared can be especially restorative. For example, for someone who is dying, having a group of friends surround that person's bed and offer symbols of or words about what the dying person means to them blesses them all and may help the one who is dying move on in their journey. Or gathering by a stream together while the ashes of the deceased are poured into it and everyone sings a song of blessing both supports and empowers those who are grieving.

Recognizing the need for rituals that both embrace and go beyond traditional faith practices, several authors provide excellent resources for thinking about how to create meaningful rituals and examples of rituals you may use. Some of these resources are listed in the Appendix.

Whether using a ritual created by someone else or developing your own, whenever possible the ritual should be developed in consultation with the person you are supporting. What sacred symbols, actions, and words are meaningful to them? What kind of connection with the Holy do they hope to achieve through this ritual, and how? How might you invite God into the sacred space, and how will you involve those seeking healing so they can experience God's presence? Godward listening will help you both discern what needs to be expressed and blessed through the ritual, and what symbols and actions will best do that.

Your Self

One of my finest teachers told us pastors-in-training repeatedly: "You are your tool for ministry." What she meant was that what you have to work with in your caregiving first and foremost are your own skills, knowledge, emotional health, and spiritual presence. That means you must be continually attentive to your cognitive understandings of, feelings about, and faith responses to death and dying.

Self-Awareness

You need to be aware of what is going on inside yourself as you are preparing to offer care, are in the midst of that care, and after you have offered care. That does not mean an obsessive self-focus on "what about me?" in your work. That would detract from your ability to be present to others. It does mean paying attention, checking in regularly with yourself, noticing what you are thinking, feeling, and experiencing spiritually. It means asking yourself questions like, "What was it about this particular death that made me feel so angry?" "What is it about this care-receiver that worries me about being able to offer him effective care?"

It is important to know this: if you have recently lost a loved one and are in the midst of your own grief process, this may not be the time to be learning about end-of-life care (although many people enter ministry at such a time, as a way, although usually unconsciously, of helping themselves heal). Rather, you need to care for yourself right now and find pastoral supporters who can care for you in your loss. Later, when you have healed and are ready to move forward, you may want to become such a caregiver.

You can be present to yourself and to others only if you are whole and healthy. So let us consider some ways in which you can nurture your own wholeness and health and refill the spiritual reservoir from which you minister to others.

Nurturing Your Spirituality

The word "spirituality" means different things to different people. Here it refers to your connection with God and all the ways you nurture, experience, and express that connection. For most caregivers, this involves some kind of consistent spiritual practice. It may be a regular prayer-time each day. It may include regular periods of physical exercise. It may mean reading a good book or seeing a funny movie. It might involve some form of artistic expression. Virtually any practice can nurture your spirituality, as long as you engage in it with the intention of listening for and being present to the Holy through that practice.

Time and Space Away

Even Jesus took time away from his healing ministry, to rest and to refresh his relationship with God. As hard as it is to do, it is essential for you to make time and space away from your caregiving work — and you must make it, it does not simply happen. End-of-life caregiving, especially if it is your primary focus of care, is exhausting. Even with very good boundaries, good skills, and a strong faith, over time you will find yourself depleted physically, emotionally, and spiritually.

My own practice involves regular journaling, playing with my dogs and horses, and making retreats at least twice a year. One of my colleagues is an avid bicyclist, who nurtures her spirit with both short and extended bike trips. Another is a potter and nurtures herself and her relationship with God through the firm kneading of damp clay. Still another seeks out the solace of a mountain-stream with his fly-rod in hand.

Choose something that nurtures you in the midst of your daily routines and something that gets you out of those routines. Take your weekly day off and your vacation days. Time and space away from your ministry setting will refresh you physically, mentally, and emotionally, and you will be a much better minister when you return.

Finding Joy

It is easy for caregivers to get very serious — too serious — about their work. If you are caring for people in end-of-life situations, you will be tempted to focus much of your energy on them and their needs. You can lose your perspective or become depressed over life's many hardships.

For balance, you must find places of joy and laughter in life. You will learn to appreciate the moments of humor that sometimes arise in caregiving and be grateful for God's appearing to you in that way. You must also learn how to find or create relationships and experiences that make you laugh.

One colleague of mine wears temporary tattoos under her clergy clothes. Another wears a Superman tee-shirt under his suit when he has an especially hard day coming up. Another reads Dave Barry essays every morning before going to work. Many others have pets that make them smile or laugh out loud! Notice what tickles you, giving you a quiet chuckle or heavy-duty belly-laugh, and cultivate that in your life.

Your Support System

It is also easy for caregivers to become insolated — the very opposite of the communal life that God calls us to. In fact, those who serve God best appear to be people who value and enjoy rich relationships both inside and outside of their work settings.

If you have a family, tend to those relationships with the same enthusiasm and passion and interest you bring to your caregiving. Make time with your spouse or partner. Play with your children. Having a quiet cup of tea with your significant other or attending your child's band concert or senior play is every bit as important as spending time with care-receivers.

Spend time with friends too. Since boundary considerations prohibit ministers from having close relationships with those they serve (e.g., with parishioners or with patients), it may take a little work to make friendships in settings outside your work. Join the local art center or birdwatchers group or hiking club. You need friends with whom you can play or just hang out, and you need soul-friends with whom you can share your deepest concerns, and who can hold you in your hardest struggles.

Finally, develop a professional support network for yourself. This may include a psychotherapist if you are working on life-issues or a spiritual director to provide you with spiritual encouragement. A colleague group is also important, although it does not have to consist solely of clergy colleagues. It does help if the group includes people in similar lines of work with whom you can share your ideas and concerns, people with whom you can meet regularly to provide a sounding board and clinical supervision for each other. One of the greatest blessings in my life is a group of clergywomen that meets once a month, to laugh and cry together, to process questions we have about our ministries, and to share prayer and other spiritual encouragement. You may have to seek out such supports, but your ministry and your wider life will be blessed by your doing so.

Chapter Five

Pastoral Care for the Dying

O Lord, do not rebuke me in your anger,
or discipline me in your wrath.
Be gracious to me, O Lord, for I am languishing;
O Lord, heal me, for my bones are shaking with terror.
My soul also is struck with terror,
while you, O Lord — how long?
Turn, O Lord, save my life;
deliver me for the sake of your steadfast love.
— Psalm 6:1–4

Struck with Terror

Tom was fifty-two years old, in excellent health, and happily married to Akiko, his wife of twenty-four years. Their daughter had just been admitted to graduate studies at Princeton, and their high school junior son was taking his award-winning project to the National Science Fair. Tom's career was successful, and he had just earned his pilot's license after years of preparation and practice.

At Akiko's insistence, Tom went to see his family physician because he was having an intermittent fever and night sweats and he felt drained of energy. He thought he had just been working too hard and was shocked when, after some blood tests, the doctor told him he had lymphoma. Tom had always been a health-nut and was sure the doctor was mistaken.

Subsequent tests showed his cancer was the highly aggressive form of lymphoma and was already far-developed. The doctor said they could try chemotherapy treatments, but given the advanced stage of Tom's disease, things did not look hopeful. She suggested Tom get his affairs in order since he probably only had a short time to live.

Understandably, Tom was confused and angry. His anguish and his cries were those of the psalmist, his "bones" and his soul "struck with terror." How could this happen? Why now? What does it mean to be dying? Can or will God "save my life"?

Nearing the End

We are all dying, beginning the moment we are born. This chapter focuses on people and situations when death is imminent rather than coming at some unknown time in the future. We will focus here on concerns of those who are dying and in the next chapter on the concerns of their family and other loved ones. We will also consider how you may effectively minister to them in this difficult time.

You will find some overlap between some of the ideas covered in this chapter and the next. Often your care for a dying person will help also their loved ones. Sometimes your support of those struggling loved ones will provide comfort, support, or assistance to the one who is dying. And their lives often become so inter-twined that it is not always clear where care for one stops and the other begins.

One Trajectory for Dying

In 1969, Dr. Elisabeth Kübler-Ross published a landmark book called *On Death and Dying.*[18] Based on her work with terminally ill patients, she proposed a model of five emotional stages passed through by people who knew they were dying and were grieving their impending deaths.

The first stage, *denial,* occurs when a person learns he or she is dying. It may be a logical response to what seems unbelievable and an instinctive way of protecting oneself emotionally. In our opening story, Tom is shocked at his diagnosis and sure that his doctor is wrong — both are forms of denial.

Next, as the reality of their impending death registers, perhaps because symptoms worsen or because the second or third opinion sought verifies the initial diagnosis, the person often enters the stage of *anger*. The dying person may rage at her or his situation, at its apparent injustice, at themselves, at God, or at all the above. Tom may be angry because, having taken good care of himself, he doesn't "deserve" to have cancer — or because he will never see his children in the fullness of their futures.

As the anger begins to subside, dying persons may begin *bargaining*. They may promise God that if God will cure them, they will become better people, or start doing good things for others, or somehow change their life. Not only may Tom wonder if God will help him, he may make promises to try to convince God to do so.

These three stages are normal and can facilitate healing. Much research has shown that persons who resist their illness and fight for their survival are more likely to extend their life expectancy.

As the dying process extends, particularly when treatments are unavailable or ineffective, dying persons often enter the stage of *depression*. They may feel hopeless or helpless, filled with sadness and despair. Finally, with appropriate care, support, and encouragement, they may come to terms with their impending death, as they move into the *acceptance* stage.

Kübler-Ross's work was tremendously important in furthering our understandings of the complexity of the dying process and of ways to help and support dying people. However, her model also has some limitations.

First, it quickly became clear that not all dying people go through the five stages she posited, and if they do, they don't always go through the stages in her proposed order. Many people move back and forth between stages or skip some stages altogether. Some people intellectualize what is happening to them rather than attending to their feelings, on which the model focuses. Some people welcome their impending deaths and experience relief and gratitude rather than distress. Even when persons do experience some or all of Kübler-Ross's stages, their actual presentation of the stages and movement through them seem determined by many factors, including their cultural and family backgrounds. Thus, for many dying people, the model does not apply very well.

Second, many caregivers were so delighted to have a model to help facilitate their work with the dying that they quickly reframed the model from a description of the way the dying process *could* be to the way it *should* be. Ideas like having a "good death" emerged. Such a death entailed reaching acceptance, the absence of pain, completing one's "unfinished business," and achieving satisfactory relationships with loved ones. While well intentioned, concepts like "good death" can interfere with good caregiving, especially if caregivers hold standards of what a good death is and try to coerce or impel the dying person to achieve it.

The reality is that life and death are not so tidy. Many people die in considerable physical, spiritual, or mental pain. Some never acknowledge the fact that their death is looming. Some never reconcile with others or with their situation and die still angry about a family conflict from long ago or feeling cheated by life. So while it is well to be aware of emotions and behaviors that many dying people may experience, the key to effective caregiving is to be open to whatever the individual is experiencing in his or her own unique dying.

Experiences of the Dying Person

That said, there are some commonalities in the experiences of most dying care-receivers. First and foremost, they will experience loss and grief. This and other emotions described in this section are also encountered by their loved ones.

Depending on their particular circumstances, they may experience losses like those described in chapter 2. In addition, they may lose their ability to think clearly or to make good decisions, especially if they are taking pain medications. If so, they also lose their ability to participate in making decisions about their own care, including whether or not to pursue life-sustaining options.

If they are parents with younger children, they may lose their ability to physically care for them. For example, no longer able to prepare meals for, or to dress, or to play with their children, their sense of self as a good mother or father diminishes. If they become unable to work, they may lose their sense of being a contributing member to their own family or to society.

If they are children, they may lose deeply important relationships, especially if they are unable to play with their siblings or friends or attend school. They may lose their sense of well-being or of security. They may feel terrible from their treatments. They also sense their family members' emotional pain and may worry that they are its cause.

The dying must also face the loss of every person they hold dear. They may worry about loved ones who are dependent on them, grieve the future of children or grandchildren that they will not share, despair over the loss of future plans and hopes with those they cherish. And they face the ending of their existence as they know it here on Earth. Daily, each and every one of these losses brings its own kind of pain and grief.

Not surprisingly, those who are dying may feel sad, depressed, angry, or fearful at different times. They may feel cheated of the chance to accomplish certain things or frustrated by the lack of effective medical treatments for their condition. They are likely (although this is not always true) to feel a deepened need to be connected with others, to know they are not dying alone. And as we will see below, they may have a deep need for reconciliation.

On the other hand, some dying people experience a deepened appreciation of life. They may become more grateful for what they still have in their living. In spite of their pain or distress, they may become acutely aware of the gifts that each day brings. As one man put it, "I really hate what my body is doing to me, but I find joy every single morning when I wake up and see my wife's head on the pillow next to me."

Only the individual who is dying can tell you what her process is like, what is happening for him, and what kind of help (if any) they need to deal with that. Your pastoral task is to be there, to be aware, and to be open to what is happening.

Pain

The greatest fear of many who know they are dying is pain. People are often more frightened of physical suffering than they are of death itself.

For many at the end of their lives, increasing pain is a reality. However, much has been learned in recent decades about both the physiological and the psychological aspects of pain. With modern medications, many physicians assert that pain can almost always be alleviated and it is unnecessary for a person to suffer physically. That said, with progressive diseases (like cancer) pain medications may need to be changed periodically to maintain good pain relief. For some patients, it may be necessary to sacrifice a high level of awareness for physical relief or comfort, but for many dying people, that is an acceptable trade-off.

One of the great gifts of the hospice movement is its commitment to palliative care, which focuses on pain relief, comfort, and enhanced quality of life. Based on a patient's condition — for example, for cancer patients, the location of the primary tumor and the extent to which it has spread — hospice staff can make reasoned expectations about the kinds of pain that can be anticipated and provide appropriate interventions for it.

They understand that if physical pain is not managed, patients may be unable to deal with other aspects of their dying. So, they work with each patient to address their physical, emotional and spiritual pain and distress.

Key Spiritual Needs

As we saw in chapter 3, people dealing with end-of-life situations often interpret what is happening to them in a spiritual or religious way, and their questions often express a need for meaning, hope, and connection. Earlier, we discussed these concepts theologically. Now we turn to their implications for pastoral care.

Meaning

People who feel their lives have had no purpose or little impact may be deeply distressed about their dying. Those dying prematurely (e.g., children, teens, young adults) may agonize that they have not accomplished anything significant. Caregivers can help them reflect on their assumptions about this and perhaps help them realize that they have had more impact than they may recognize. You can help them consider things they have done, events they have witnessed, history of which they have been a part, with an eye to the roles they did play and why and how that matters.

Care-receivers often want to find meaning in their act of dying as well. Most want to die in ways that are consistent with their self-identity. For example, a person who has always lived a highly controlled life will want as much control over her dying as possible. Another person whose life has focused on service to others will want his death to serve others in some way if possible. You can help each person for whom you care identify what is important to them, and try to help them accomplish their goals in their dying process.

In their struggles to find meaning, care-receivers' spiritual beliefs may be very important. As they ask "why" questions, their faith beliefs may be helpful (e.g., "I don't understand why I have COPD, but I trust that God will help me through this") or unhelpful (e.g., "God must be punishing me for my drinking by giving me liver cancer"). Compassionate caregiving helps them explore and struggle with the meanings that most concern them.

Hope

Most people need assurance that in some way their lives will continue after death. There are many ways that can happen. For example, life extends through values transmitted to one's children, through artistic or other personal creations, through bequests to valued causes or organizations, or through the continuity of groups of which they have been a part.

A process like a life review can be helpful.[19] Dying persons are helped to tell their story, with a focus on interpreting and integrating their life experiences. By remembering, reflecting on, and reworking memories, they may come to value their life in new ways, find new levels of meaning in it, and discern what they hope to pass on to others. It can help them recollect the significant ways they have participated in the world and reassure them that their contributions (and so, their lives) won't be forgotten.

Encouraging engagement in hospice can also be useful. As one hospice spiritual caregiver explained, "Hospice is not about death — it's about life. It is one of the ways you can remind people you love them . . . that it's not about giving up, or admitting there is nothing else you can do, but about hoping, choosing, recognizing there are things you can do, like managing symptoms and controlling pain. . . . It's about living as well and richly as you can while you are living."[20] One of the mottos of many hospice organizations, resonant with our Christian faith, is that there is always hope — perhaps not for cure, but certainly for healing.

For many Christians, hope is found in the resurrection of Jesus Christ. Conversations about dying persons' understandings of resurrection and what they hope for in the life hereafter can help them move forward with a sense of reassurance and peaceful expectation.

Connection

The dying often feel lonely because, realistically, they are left alone by many who care about them. Family members or friends may feel uncomfortable visiting the dying because they feel they don't know what to say — or because it is too frightening for them to experience such inescapable images of their own mortality. Helping family members be with and say good-bye to their loved ones will be healing for both.

There is also a growing recognition among professional care-givers of how essential continued community is to the dying. One of the great gifts of the hospice movement has been to ensure that the dying are not abandoned. In addition, many hospitals and nursing homes provide ways for loved ones to stay with the dying, offering family sleeping and dining facilities and sometimes day-care as well. These arrangements allow loved ones to be together to the very end.

In one excellent long-term care facility for persons with demen-tia, when a resident was actively dying, his or her bed would be moved into the center of the communal living-space so that other residents could come and touch the dying person gently, and say good-bye, each in their own way. This was clearly very healing both for the persons dying and for those about to lose them.

As pastoral caregiver, you too add a unique presence. As you companion dying people, you provide not only a loving human presence, but the reminder that God is with them too.

You can also assist with reconciliation. This nearly always involves the ability to forgive others, oneself, or both. When the dying person has been harmed, intentionally or inadvertently by another, this forgiveness can be very difficult. It is help-ful, although sometimes not possible, if the offender is willing to acknowledge her or his wrongdoing in the relationship. At the very least, open discussion about what happened can be an important step toward healing.

Even harder can be the forgiveness of oneself for something done long ago, perhaps with the best of intentions, which led to a rift in relationship. Often those who are dying will express their profound regret and grief over something they did in the past that damaged their relationship with someone important to them. For example, the father who disowned his son when his son disclosed that he was gay, or the wife who divorced her husband because of his extra-marital relationship. Open-ended questions like, "What would you like to tell him now?" or "If you could get a message to him today, what would you like him to know?" can help people move toward reconciliation, even with a person no longer in their life.

Helpful care, when dying persons are conscious, often involves assisting them in realistically examining their own role and responsibility in what happened in the past, and the role and responsibility of others. It also involves helping them reflect on their understandings of both human and divine forgiveness and how that is extended to them and to others.

The Four Things

Hospice physician Ira Byock encourages his patients to say what he calls "the four things" to others they care about: Please forgive me. I forgive you. Thank you. I love you. He has found that even in relationships where there has been profound hurt, deep healing can occur if dying persons and their loved ones can say the four things to each other.[21]

Theologically, the four things facilitate finding meaning and accomplishing reconciliation. Helping care-receivers reflect on and express their forgiveness of others, their need for forgiveness, their gratitude, and their love, in whatever form each of these might take, affirms their connections to others, and the sacredness of their living and their dying. It also helps them say good-bye in a way that blesses them and those they love.

Even when dying persons are unconscious and apparently unaware, considerable evidence suggests that when others make amends or take some action to facilitate closure, there is some level of awareness that resolution has been achieved. So it is helpful to encourage loved ones to speak to the dying, expressing their feelings and perhaps sharing their gratitude for what they appreciate about the one they are losing. My experience and that of many other caregivers indicates that those messages are received at some deep level and can be a final gift of peace-giving to the one who is dying.

Special Cases

Dying Children

Up until the twentieth century, infant, child, and adult mortality rates were high. Many children did not live to adolescence. With improved disease prevention, nutrition, and health care for many, life expectancy has increased and fewer children die. Even so, depending on your ministry, you may be called to care for a dying child and her or his family.

Although family members may be in denial or trying to keep a terminal diagnosis secret from the child, most terminally ill children know that they are dying. They may tell their favorite aunt (or pastor), "Don't let Mommy know that I know I'm going to die because it will make her sad." They are aware of their own physical pain, of the treatments they are receiving, and most important, of their own feelings and the feelings experienced by those around them.

Although children's understandings of death may be different from those of adults, most caregiving professionals believe it is important for family members and other caregivers to be honest with little ones in age-appropriate ways. Letting children express their feelings, including their fears, also provides the chance to reassure them that those who love them will be there for them in the ways they most need.

Like adults, dying children need to grieve what they have already lost and what they are going to lose. They need a chance to wonder aloud about their own spiritual questions, like, "Are you going to get a new little boy after I die?" (Does my life have meaning?), "What will happen after I die?" (Is there hope?), and "Who's going to take care of me if I have another operation?" (Do I have connection?).

While pastoral care for dying children can be especially heart-wrenching, it is deeply important to do well. As pastoral caregiver, you may be the one person able to calmly be with them, openly hear them, and bravely accompany them on their journey.

Persons with AIDS

Until very recently, people with the diseases of leprosy, tuberculo-sis, or cancer suffered almost as much from social stigma as from their disease. Although decreasing in some geographic areas, we see a similar stigma attached to persons with HIV or AIDS and sometimes to their loved ones.

AIDS and HIV are increasing dramatically in the United States and in other countries. In this country, the first hundred thousand cases were recorded in the ten years between 1980 and the end of that decade. The second hundred thousand cases were recorded in the next two years. Since the year 2000, rates of incidence continue to grow in many populations, especially among the elderly. As a pastoral caregiver in almost any setting, you will almost certainly be working with persons who are living or dying with AIDS.

Contrary to many stereotypes, AIDS patients come in all ages, ethnicities, sexual orientations, and other circumstances. Babies contract the disease from infected mothers. Teens contract it from sex with an infected person or through IV drug use. Straight people contract it from sexual intimacies with an infected loved one, through shared needle use, or through blood transfusions (though this is increasingly uncommon). Gay people contract it the same way. The person to whom you offer care may be ten years old, twenty-five years old, fifty-five years old, gay, straight, bisexual, well- or poorly educated, affluent or poor.

Despite their differences, people living or dying with AIDS[22] share common care needs. Because of the stigma the disease still conveys, they may be abandoned by others, facing their dying alone at the time they most need support and care. They may be shunned by their own family members or abandoned by the person who infected them. They may have to deal with anger or guilt related to how they were infected. They may suffer frustration and anger if their physician or other health-care professionals decline to treat them. They may be worried financially, as their insurance benefits may be terminated or inadequate to cover the cost of their medications or other care.

When these difficult and painful experiences occur, the pastoral caregiver may be the only person willing to provide ongoing support for such dying persons and their loved ones. The good news is that pastoral caregivers like you are increasingly better-informed about the disease and its effects, and so are better able to offer excellent care.

Offering Pastoral Care

We have already considered many things you can do to be helpful. Be there. Don't be afraid. Or at least don't let your fear get in the way of the process. Listen. Let go of your expectations about what should happen. Accept (don't judge) what is or isn't happening. Respect the process. Stay in relationship. Don't worry about doing great things; do "small things with great love," as Mother Teresa said. Let silence happen. Be grateful they are letting you travel with them.

Stories — Again

As we saw in chapter 4, biblical stories can be powerful tools for healing. Just as important are the stories of care-receivers' lives. So another significant gift you can offer the dying is to help them tell — and compassionately listen to — their life-stories.

Let them teach you about their past and about their present. After all, they are the only ones who know what this experience is like for them — and how it fits into the wider context of their whole life. Your curiosity and interest help care-receivers reflect on their lives with the possibility for discovering new wisdom, including the crucial understanding that whatever shape their lives have had, whatever choices they have made, their lives have indeed been meaningful — which, at bottom, is perhaps what dying people want to know most of all.

Not all those who want to will be able to share their story because of physical or mental incapacity. As death nears, persons may be heavily medicated, unable to speak, or unconscious. Even in these situations, it can be helpful for family members, if they are able, to reminisce aloud about "the Christmas when . . . " or "that trip to . . ." One family, gathered at the bedside of their dying father (who had been comatose for several days), was sharing some of their treasured memories. Suddenly, the father opened his eyes, said quite clearly, "That was a great summer, wasn't it?" then closed his eyes, and died a short time later. He had "heard" the story, and been blessed by it.

Family members and friends may not be able to do this because of the pain it causes them. It may be too hard for them to listen to wonderful old memories because they are already grieving as they lose this relationship, or to listen to unhappy tales from the past because they "just don't want to go through that old stuff all over again." As pastoral caregiver, your open, nonjudgmental ear and heart can offer the dying person a deeply needed opportunity for connection, for confession, for reconciliation, and for peaceful acceptance of what has been and what is yet to come.

Know that not everyone will want to share their story. Persons who are intensely private, ashamed, afraid they will be judged, or badly wounded may be unable or unwilling to talk about their experience and may find even a gentle invitation to do so invasive. Good caregiving honors those feelings and preferences too, rather than trying to compel care-receivers to tell you more than they wish to. What is needed is your ability to accept all persons as they are, to help elicit and listen to their story if they want to tell it, and to respectfully walk alongside them however they will allow you to do that.

Getting Information

Another important pastoral task may be helping care-receivers get information they need. Very ill people are often heavily medicated, frightened, and badly stressed. They and their families may have little understanding of what is happening to them. Busy medical staff may not make time to explain procedures, options, or prognoses in a way that patients or families can fully comprehend.

While HIPAA regulations prohibit medical staff from sharing confidential information with persons other than patients or their families, they will sometimes give you, the patient's pastor, information they believe they have given the family, but that perhaps was not comprehended. You can help care-receivers understand and process this information.

You may also help family members find needed resources, such as home health aides, housekeepers, child-care providers, and other practical-support people. While it is important for them to do as much of this as possible for themselves so they can feel empowered rather than helpless, you will often have information about resources in the community that can be helpful to them.

Finally, a caution. It is easy for some pastoral caregivers to focus on this aspect of care. It is much more comfortable to give information than to be a pastorally present listener and companion. Be attentive to the choices you make about the primary role you play as caregiver.

Don't Assume

Although it seems as if dying people "should" welcome pastoral care, it may not be so. As with any other area of pastoral care, if someone calls you asking you to visit someone else (in this case, a dying person), check with that person directly if possible to determine whether he or she welcomes a pastoral visit.

Sometimes you will check ahead, be invited to come, then arrive to find that the person won't talk to you. If so, remember that people who are dying may be having an especially bad day with a lot of pain or very little energy. Or they may be struggling with their own denial about their illness and unwilling to acknowledge that spiritual care could be helpful. Or the person may simply have changed her or his mind.

Try not to be hurt or offended if this happens. Ask respectfully if they would like you to return some other time. Abide by their wishes in this matter. After all, they know better than you whether they want spiritual care.

Blessings Happen

Providing presence and care to those in pain and grief takes great courage and love. If you are able to offer this kind of care (and not everyone is), it will be a real blessing to others.

Though you may find it hard to believe right now, it will also bless you. As those who are dying or struggling or mourning share their stories with you and allow you into the tenderest places in their lives, you will learn more about mystery, life, the Holy, and yourself than you can imagine. At the end of each such journey you make with another, not only will they be transformed, you will be too.

Chapter Six

Pastoral Care for the Struggling

When she had said this, she went back and called her sister Mary, and told her privately, "The Teacher is here and is calling for you." And when she heard it, she got up quickly and went to him. Now Jesus had not yet come to the village, but was still at the place where Martha had met him. The Jews who were with her in the house, consoling her, saw Mary get up quickly and go out. They followed her because they thought that she was going to the tomb to weep there. When Mary came where Jesus was and saw him, she knelt at his feet and said to him, "Lord, if you had been here, my brother would not have died."

When Jesus saw her weeping, and the Jews who came with her also weeping, he was greatly disturbed in spirit and deeply moved. He said, "Where have you laid him?" They said to him, "Lord, come and see." Jesus began to weep. So the Jews said, "See how he loved him!" But some of them said, "Could not he who opened the eyes of the blind man have kept this man from dying?" —John 11:28–37

Disturbed in Spirit

Darren, a hospital chaplain, was paged to the ICU. Staff directed him to the family room, where the family of a dying patient waited. As he entered the room, he could feel waves of anger and discord filling the room. An older woman sat weeping on a couch, with a middle-aged woman sitting with her, patting her shoulder. Another woman sat nearby, and a third was pacing nervously. Occasionally, the older woman looked up and glared at two burly middle-aged men who stood in the middle of the small room, arguing loudly.

Darren introduced himself and was told that Macon, the family patriarch, was in renal failure. Macon had stopped breathing on his own some time before, and at the request of the older son had been placed on a respirator that was now keeping him alive. The increasingly violent argument was over whether to respect their mother's wishes to "just let your dad go and stop his suffering," or to keep him alive regardless, the wish of the older brother. Finally, tempers snapped completely, and one brother swung at the other's head, with Darren stepping between them to try to stop the fight.

Strugglers

In both the Gospel story and the ICU story, we see people struggling with the terrible pain of loss. Martha and Mary have lost their beloved brother. Jesus has lost his dear friend. The ICU family members are losing a cherished husband and father.

In the Gospel story, Mary and the wider crowd are sorrow-filled and angry and blame Jesus for not having arrived sooner to prevent Lazarus's death. In the ICU, the brothers are angry and blaming each other for not really knowing what to do. When the end of life approaches or arrives, people are hurting, questioning, and struggling to figure out what to do and how to be in this terrible time.

Webster's definitions of "struggle" include: "to contend with an opponent"; "to make great efforts or attempts"; "to labor"; and "to make one's way with difficulty." Each of these accurately describes those linked physically and/or emotionally to a person who is dying.

They are contending both with the unknowns that death proffers and the knowns of the current painful situation, are often laboring very hard to meet the unending needs of the person they love, and are making their way with difficulty. Thus, the term "strugglers" will be used here to describe and recognize them, as we consider some of the challenges with which they are contending, and how pastoral caregivers may be able to help them.

Common Experiences

Like those for whom they care, strugglers may be experiencing denial, anger, anxiety, guilt, or depression. They too may bargain with God or rage against accepting what is happening. They are experiencing their own losses and their own grief.

Spouses and partners are losing the daily companionship of and shared experiences with their significant other. Home-keeping, child-rearing, play and leisure joys become the sole task of the struggler. Parents of dying children lose their sense of competence and effectiveness as a parent, and their hopes and dreams for their child's future. Young children losing parents or siblings lose their sense of security and safety in the world. Adult children losing aging parents lose their sense of rootedness and continuity.

For those providing direct care, there is a loss of physical energy and well-being as those are expended on behalf of their loved ones. The struggler's own nutritional and rest needs are usually set aside to care for the person dying. If finances are stretched, the struggler's own needs for health care or medications may go unmet.

Emotionally, they may become increasingly isolated as friends stop visiting, and all of their own time and energy is focused on the needs of the person dying. They too are anguished, both by the suffering their loved one may be experiencing and by the certain knowledge that they are about to lose someone they love dearly. And they face a future that will be forever changed by the loss of this person.

They lose their "normal" life of activities, independence, joy, and anticipation and must struggle with the realities that make up their new "normal." They often lose financial security as their resources are drained by the costs of medications and treatments. They may even lose their sense of faith as they wonder where God is in what is happening, and why God has not fixed things and cured this beloved person. Their wounded cry is that of Mary and Martha to Jesus: "Where have you been, and why didn't you stop this from happening?"

Each of these losses — and there are many more — brings grief. So pastoral caregivers may need to help them with both practical assistance and with their grieving both before and after death occurs.

Common Needs

The particular kind of care a struggler needs will depend on many factors. One is the relationship between the struggler and the person dying. When one is losing a spouse or partner, the losses are different from when one is losing a sibling. When one is losing a child, the losses are different from those when one loses a significant adult. Second, the circumstances of the one who is dying may affect the struggler's grief process. If a loved one has been ill and in considerable distress for a long period of time, it may (although it is not always so) be easier to say good-bye to them than when one receives a sudden unexpected diagnosis and the dying process is very short. And, the emotional and financial resources available play a large role in determining the struggler's requisites. As is true in all caregiving, your task is to listen carefully to determine what it is this particular struggler needs in your work together.

Practical Supports

When dying people are seriously ill, strugglers may need concrete supports from other caregivers. Hospice teams, for example, can assist with medications, dressing changes, obtaining needed medical supplies and equipment, and connecting the struggler with other needed services. Home health aides offer other options and may let the dying person stay at home rather than requiring hospitalization or a nursing home. The struggler's faith community or social communities may also be able to help with meals, babysitting, or sitting with the sick person so the caregiver can have some time away. Often people will be delighted to help if they just know what needs doing. You can assist strugglers in clarifying what they need. They are often so overwhelmed that is a hard thing to do. You can also connect strugglers with those who can help meet their needs.

Belonging

Strugglers need caring community most at the same time that others are most likely to abandon them because others "don't know what to say" or what to do to help. If possible, remind their congregation that prayer support is important, as are notes, cards, and visits (if the struggler welcomes visitors). If you are a parish pastor, it is a great service both to strugglers and to parishioners to teach them how to provide appropriate support and to make helpful visits. For most people, it is uncomfortable at first; over time, everyone will experience the deep blessings that occur.

As pastoral caregiver, you will want to be respectful of the boundaries set by strugglers. Not all of them will welcome phone calls or visits, preferring their privacy. Hopefully, they will make this clear to you. To whatever degree they allow, it will be immensely helpful for you to maintain an active interest in both the sick person and the strugglers and to keep in regular contact.

Time Away

Unless you have cared for someone who is gravely ill, it is hard to understand how utterly draining it is, even though the caregiver may love the dying person very much. Because of that love, many strugglers don't want to leave the person they are caring for, or take time for themselves. They may resist any suggestions you or others make about getting assistance or making some time away from their loved one.

For their own well-being, it is important to encourage them to do so, even if it is only to take a daily walk, or to have a weekly lunch out with friends. You may also need to be creative in helping them find ways to do this crucial self-care.

Spiritual Needs

Like those for whom they care, strugglers also need to find meaning, hope, and connection. They need to know that the care they are offering and the sacrifices they are making matter, and reassurance that they are doing everything possible for their loved one. They need to know that things will get better, even if that does not mean their loved one will be cured. And they need to be reminded that they are a valued and loved member of the community. Because you represent the God who loves and holds us and who promises that all things are possible, they may find your reassurances about these matters especially meaningful and consoling.

Special Cases

While every death is unique, there are some situations that raise unique concerns for strugglers. This chapter will address some of those needs. Resources in the Appendix cover these special situations in greater depth.

Parents of Dying Children

As infant mortality has decreased and life expectancy has increased, we have come to believe that almost everyone born will survive to a ripe old age. As a rule, parents expect their children to outlive them. (The exception involves families struggling with poverty and marginalization, who are well aware of the fragility of their children's lives.) So when a child is diagnosed with a terminal illness, it is shattering for parents. One of the most agonizing forms of struggle is that of a parent caring for a dying child.

They may have difficulty talking about what is happening with the child — and with their other children. This may be because of their own denial about the child's impending death or their wish to maintain hope or their desire to make the last days of their child's life as happy as possible. They may need help understanding what their child is likely experiencing. For example, children have less "unfinished business" that needs attending. Their ideas about dying seem less anxiety-producing. They don't feel a need to pretend everything is okay or to hide their feelings.

What dying children do need is to be encouraged to express all of their feelings, including their frustrations and anger about being ill, their fears about dying, their feeling cheated by not being able to accomplish certain goals. They may also need the opportunity to fulfill some long-held goal or dream and be able to convey particular messages to their various family members.

Some children may also want a say in whether painful treatments should be continued and where they wish to die. Teens may want to help make funeral plans. When there have been broken relationships in a family, as with divorce, they may need contact and reconciliation with their noncustodial parent.

While parents are struggling to meet these many needs, they often must also attend to the needs of other children. This includes helping those children understand what is happening, creating ways for siblings to say good-bye to one another, encouraging them to express their feelings, and continuing to meet their daily needs for care and nurture.

In the face of so many demands and needs, it's no wonder that parents are often physically and emotionally exhausted. At a time when self-care is so important, they are least likely to do it.

Pastoral caregivers can help provide a context in which both parents and children feel free to speak their feelings and express their needs. You may also encourage parents to draw on help from other family members, friends, and professionals. You can help the whole family acknowledge that the end is nearing, name what will help them find meaning in their final days together, and perhaps help them accomplish those final tasks.

Children Facing a Loved One's Death

How do children and teens respond when a parent or sibling is dying? What do they think, and how do they feel? And how can pastoral caregivers be of help?

Research on children's understandings of death indicates that the way they and teens understand dying and death depends on their age and stage of cognitive and social development. Very young children believe that death is like sleep, and is temporary. Slightly older children often personify death as a powerful monster that can be outwitted or escaped with the proper strategy. Children nearing adolescence begin to realize that death is both inescapable and permanent.

Whatever their intellectual understandings, children do sense the emotional impact of death. They understand that death is serious, and when someone dies, they feel deeply sad. Children are also highly attuned to the feelings of adults around them. Even when those adults refuse to talk about Daddy's cancer or pretend that everything is going to be okay, children can feel the anxiety, fear, and pain of those well-intentioned grown-ups. They may be even more frightened or distressed because they know they aren't being told the truth. In fact, most professionals who work with children and teens agree that if someone they love is dying — or if they themselves are terminally ill — children know that.

So children need age-appropriate honest answers to their questions. As is true for most adults, kids can cope far better when they have trustworthy information. They also need a chance to honestly express their feelings and have those feelings accepted and validated. And they need to be reassured that they are loved and won't be abandoned. Children are totally dependent on their parents for care and nurture and need to know they will still be cared for even if Mommy or Daddy dies.

Caregivers for People Who Have Dementia

In the last few decades, with improved medical technology and care increasing average life spans, the incidence of Alzheimer's disease and other dementias has increased tremendously. While the exact number of dementia patients in the United States is unknown, estimates range from two to eight million people. Millions more people love them and are struggling to care for them.

So as a pastoral caregiver, you will almost certainly be working with persons in these situations.

Although Alzheimer's is a fatal disease, generally patients with this or other forms of dementia are not considered "terminal," since the course of their disease usually lasts anywhere from three to twenty years after diagnosis. Even so, as the disease progresses, those who love them experience emotional, social, and spiritual "deaths" and need care similar to that for carers for other dying people.

Caring for a person with dementia is exhausting physically and emotionally, and draining financially. Persons with the disease lose the ability to communicate, to share jokes, to enjoy activities together, to do all those things that make up the fabric of relationships — often lifelong relationships. In addition, while those stricken can receive emotional messages from others, they often lose their ability to return those messages, leaving their spouses, partners, or adult children feeling lonely and bereft. Finally, depending on their awareness of their own disease, they may struggle with pronounced fearfulness, confusion, anxiety, or anger.

Caregivers become responsible for answering endlessly repeated questions, soothing fears that may not seem to make any sense, trying to make the ill adult bathe or put on clean clothes, shopping for food, preparing meals, and doing all the housework, some of which they may never have done before. Over time they will be caring for a person who may no longer recognize them. Strugglers may say, "I'm mourning because I've lost my wife (or husband or partner) even though physically she (or he) is still right here with me." Strugglers often become isolated as they increasingly stay at home with the demented person, deeply depressed, and likely to suffer severe health consequences of their own.

Your role as pastoral caregiver is to support both the care-receivers and the caregivers. All of your skills, knowledge, and creativity may be called into play.

If you care for people with dementia, it is important to talk to them, assuming they may understand, even if that is not apparent.

Gentle appropriate touch is also soothing, especially for people who are seldom touched by anyone who is not changing their clothing or doing other physical care. Praying with them, reading Scripture, singing old hymns, and sharing Communion can be deeply meaningful.

Care for strugglers is equally important. Anything you can do to encourage them to care for themselves is important. Champion their use of practical community resources like Meals on Wheels, support their continuing church attendance or participation in local service organizations or hobby groups, including helping them find care for their loved ones so they can be safely left for a short while. Attending a caregivers' support group specifically for them is invaluable. And simply listening to what is happening and faithfully witnessing to their despair and grief is a great gift.

Caregivers for People With AIDS

As discussed in chapter 5, in many communities, AIDS carries a social stigma. So it raises special concerns for strugglers whose loved ones have the disease.

Depending on the source of infection, strugglers may feel intensely angry or hurt. Parents of sons with AIDS may learn for the first time that their son is gay. Parents of an infected teenaged daughter may learn that she has been engaging in recreational IV drug use. The wife infected by her husband (or vice versa) may feel agonizingly betrayed.

Strugglers may also feel guilty that they didn't somehow protect their loved one better. They may feel bitter toward those who have imperiled their loved one's life. They may feel angry at God or at the apparent injustice of life. And as with all life-threatening situations, they may feel intense grief.

These feelings can be exacerbated if strugglers and those for whom they care experience outright discrimination from medical personnel and other professionals, or if they suffer financially when insurance companies refuse to provide appropriate coverage. Overall, these strugglers may also experience more extreme abandonment and isolation than any other caregivers.

Clearly they have a deep need for pastoral support — and may be least likely to receive it. Despite Jesus' warnings about judging others, some Christians still view this disease as a moral rather than biological consequence. Many faith communities continue to perpetuate myths and stereotypes about the disease and its sufferers, sometimes adding the theological judgment that "it is a punishment from God." While such judgments are unfaithful to the Gospel, and erroneous scientifically and sociologically, they still abound. As pastoral caregiver, you may need to wrestle with your own understandings and those of your faith community with regard to these issues and determine whether agape or judgment will have higher priority as you provide care in these situations.

Fortunately, this is beginning to change, with some congregations developing care ministries specifically for persons with AIDS or HIV and their caregivers. In Houston, for example, a huge ecumenical AIDS Interfaith Council initiates and supports caregiving programs for thousands affected by the disease. In Denver, a UMC-based meal program provides nutritious lunches and dinners to patients and caregivers. Learning what is available in your community, at the congregational, county, or regional level will help you build bridges between your care-receivers' needs and those resources.

The Hardest Decision

Stephen was a thirty-two-year-old man, beloved by his family and many friends, dying from an inoperable brain tumor. One effect of the tumor was increasing confusion, which often left him terrified, agitated, and unable to sleep. He became increasingly upset and unable to communicate with his family. Ruth was an eighty-four-year-old woman, beloved by her longtime companion, Bill, hospitalized first for heart surgery, then kept in the hospital for complications that arose. She could not regain her strength; after six weeks of small strokes, she lapsed into a coma. Fred was a fifty-year-old man who had made huge career sacrifices to help his talented athletic son train for the Olympics. Fred's sudden short-ness of breath was diagnosed as lung cancer, which could not be treated surgically, and six months of chemotherapy proved inef-fective. It became an agonizing struggle for him to draw breath, and he daily told his family, "Please, please make this stop."

In each of these situations, loved ones were faced with the hardest decision a struggler may have to make — whether or how to let their loved one's life end. It may be a decision about which treatment procedures to elect (e.g., additional surgery, chemo-therapy, or radiation therapy) or whether to continue artificial life-support — respiratory support, nutrition, or hydration — for the person who is dying.

Too often these decisions are made during medical crises. Stephen was increasingly confused, frightened, and distressed. Ruth lost consciousness. Fred was in agonizing pain, relieved only by frequent medication. In the ICU example that began this chap-ter, the father's kidneys and other systems were shutting down. Unfortunately, none of their families had discussed their wishes ahead of time about what they would like to have happen in such circumstances. So they became embroiled in guilt and anger when decisions were forced upon them.

As a pastoral caregiver, encouraging families to discuss these decisions ahead of time can make it far easier for them to make choices that feel right for their loved one's situation when the time comes that the decisions must be made. It will serve both strug-glers and the dying person well to make these important choices when they are feeling well and cognitively and emotionally sound rather than when emotions are running high and no one is able to think clearly.

It is important, especially when a dying person has a terminal illness, for both the patient and her or his loved ones to under-stand their options. Most states require that unless the patient or family has specified otherwise, if the patient goes into cardiac arrest or other medical crisis, the medical team is required to try to resuscitate that person. If a dying care-receiver or her or his family has preferences about end-of-life care, they need to make those clear and put them in writing. Most hospitals provide guidelines and legal forms for these purposes.

Emotionally several issues usually surface. One regards quality of life. If the treatment is pursued or nutrition is continued and the person regains some function, will their quality of life be good? Importantly, will it be the quality of life the sick person would want to have?

A second issue is whether terminating life-support, especially nutrition or hydration, is going to cause the dying person greater pain or discomfort. For example, with Fred, it was clear that the quality of his present life was very poor and that his future was limited. Would discontinuing artificial nutrition make him even more miserable, or as one horrified family member put it, "You mean we're going to make him starve to death?"

You can provide more helpful support if you understand that what a gravely ill person experiences when, for example, artificial nourishment is discontinued is different from what a well person would experience. It appears that a lack of food or other liquids is not terrible or painful for those who are already near death. While we cannot totally understand the experiences of the dying, most caregivers' observations suggest that in fact neither lack of nutrition or hydration increase a terminally ill person's suffering, and it appears they actually can contribute to a more comfortable passage from this life. What usually happens is that the patients become sleepier and sleepier until they finally pass away quietly.

A third issue regards interpersonal ties. What kinds of relationships exist between the dying person and the strugglers? If there is considerable anger over past behavior, that may affect the decision one way. If there is guilt or shame about past interactions, that may affect the decision differently. Pastorally, helping all participants reflect on their relationships, and on what will best honor those relationships, will be a great service both to them and to the person who is dying.

Finally, theologically, the question most likely to arise for a struggler is, "Am I playing God by terminating life-support?" While there are many ways to argue this issue, in the view of many medical ethicists, by letting whatever needs to happen happen, one is permitting God to do what God needs to do rather than trying to intervene in that natural process.

As caregiver, you need to know what you, your faith tradition, and the care-receivers' faith tradition believes about each of these issues. If embraced or permitted, you then need to know what persons' options are. Learn what advance directives (living wills, Five Wishes, powers of attorney, and Do Not Resuscitate orders) are available in your state. Discern how you can help strugglers reflect on their choices. As in all pastoral care, it is not your job to make a decision for them, but to help them faithfully consider possibilities and to support them in whatever decision they make.

Sharing Care

Only three generations ago, if someone was dying, families stepped in to support the struggler. Grandpa picked up the kids after school, and Grandma watched them until bedtime or kept them overnight. Mom baked casseroles for her daughter's family, Uncle Sam took the car in for maintenance, and Aunt Sally took the laundry home each week.

In today's increasingly mobile society, strugglers may live half a continent away from family. So while family members still sometimes travel long distance to assist, most strugglers' needs for support are increasingly being met by organizations like local hospitals, hospices, and congregations. Online organizations like *sharethecare.org* help willing friends and neighbors organize and delegate tasks that need doing when strugglers are too overwhelmed to do so. Computer-savvy teens or friends can be recruited to provide status reports to keep others updated when strugglers are too tired to do so.

Hospice can be extraordinarily helpful. While thirty years ago, almost no one knew what hospice was, today there are hospice organizations in or near almost every community in this country. They can offer care that pastors cannot and can help us care for others more effectively. As one hospice chaplain put it, "Hospice is not about death; it's about life. Bringing in hospice is one of the ways you can remind people you love them. You are giving them all the support you can, and adding additional support. . . . A lot of family members think that bringing in hospice is about giving up, because there's nothing else you can do. But there is — hospice can help manage symptoms and alleviate pain in ways family cannot. It really is about life. . . . I wish families would bring their members in earlier — they and their loved ones would benefit so much."[23]

Hospice affirms the concept of palliative care as an intensive program that enhances comfort and promotes quality of life for individuals and their families. When cure is no longer possible, hospice recognizes that a peaceful and comfortable death is an essential goal of health care.[24] To that end, hospices provide an array of supports for the dying and the struggling.

In most communities, hospitals and human-service agencies also help with supplemental caregiving services. And for members of faith communities, their congregations can help with food needs, practical home-care, and emotional and spiritual support.

Only the struggler can determine what kind of support system he or she most needs and what will work best for his or her lifestyle, goals, schedule, and resources. "The only bad decision is not seeking support at all."[25] Pastoral caregivers can assist strugglers with identifying what their needs, goals, and current resources are and help them build bridges to people and organizations which can supply those needs.

Chapter 7

When the End Comes

*They had a long robe with sleeves taken to their father, and they
said, "This we have found; see now whether it is your son's robe
or not." He recognized it, and said, "It is my son's robe! A wild
animal has devoured him; Joseph is without doubt torn to pieces."
Then Jacob tore his garments, and put sackcloth on his loins, and
mourned for his son many days. All his sons and all his daughters
sought to comfort him; but he refused to be comforted, and said,
"No, I shall go down to Sheol to my son, mourning." Thus his
father bewailed him.*   —Genesis 37:32–35

Tearing Their Garments

In the tiny, overly warm bedroom of her house, Pearl lies dying,
covered with a faded pink chenille bedspread and a fluffy prayer
shawl from her church wrapped around her shoulders. She is
ninety and has ovarian cancer. Her two middle-aged daughters
have managed to keep her in her home, and extended family
have brought meals, sat with Pearl, and supported all three of
them through her long and painful illness.

The daughters know she is near the end of her life, fading in and
out of consciousness, and have called Pastor Paul, Pearl's minister
of nearly three decades. When he arrives, he shares a cup of coffee
with the daughters, while a grandson sits at the bedside and holds
Pearl's hand. Then the whole family gathers in the bedroom and
surrounds the bed, as Pastor Paul prays with them and helps them
say good-bye.

In the tiny waiting-room outside the E.R., a family waits. Their twenty-two-year-old daughter, recently graduated from college and headed for graduate school, has been in an accident. In spite of the frantic activity in the treatment suite, no one has come to talk to them, except to tell them that "everything possible is being done." The E.R. chaplain, Tanika Samuels, checks in with the medical team and learns that in spite of their efforts, the massive damage from the accident was simply too much to repair, and the young woman, whose whole life of promise was ahead of her, is gone.

She takes a minute to pray and center, then steps into the waiting-room. She relays the terrible news as gently as she can. No one moves. Then the father stands, strides across the room, and picks up a heavy metal garbage-can and hurls it at the chaplain, who just manages to get out of the way. Then he screams at her to "get out of here," and collapses, wailing his grief.

In the ICU, the Rev. Celia Escalona stands by the bedside of a young man named Pete, who is dying of complications from AIDS. She doesn't know Pete very well, but she does know his parents, who are parishioners in the church she serves. A few days before, Pete's condition deteriorated markedly, and he was on a respirator. The doctors have made it clear that he is not going to improve and in fact will not long survive, and asked the family to decide whether to continue life-support.

After two days of painful conversations, they have decided to let their son go but cannot bear to be with him while he dies. They have asked Celia to come and be with Pete while the life-support system is disconnected. She holds his hand and speaks softly to him as the nurse removes the tubes and equipment. She sees Pete's vitals drop on the bedside monitor, and notices his breathing begin to slow. She continues to speak to him, reminding him of his parents' deep love for him, praying aloud for him, and blessing him on his journey. Over the next twenty minutes, his breathing becomes more labored and ever-slower, and finally he ceases breathing and his heart stops beating. She offers a final blessing, then goes to his parents who are waiting outside, and holds Pete's mother as she weeps.

Care for the Dying Person

Like our Bible story, these scenarios describe the struggles of loved ones as a person passes from this life to the next. The pastoral question is, How can you help make this transition easier for the person who is dying, and for those who love that person?

Being There

Knowing what to do when someone is near death is not always easy. Even so, you may place expectations on yourself about what you "should" do or where you "should" be when someone is dying. Your ministerial training may have suggested what you "should" do and when. Colleagues may share their personal rules about what "should" happen at these times. For example, a senior colleague once told me, "As soon as I know someone is dying, I go right then. It's irresponsible to do anything else. They need you!"

As our stories illustrate, while some people will indeed need and want you there as they die (or as their loved one is dying), others will not. When someone calls to let you know that someone is dying or has just died, simply asking, "May I come?" or "Would you like me to come now, or do you want some quiet time with your family to be with all this?" is helpful. It encourages care-receivers to recognize what they need at that moment and gives them a sense of control. If they do want you to come by all means go and be with them if you can.

Beyond Physical Presence

Besides being physically present with the dying or their loved ones, you must also be emotionally and spiritually present. For example, a chaplain was called to the Birth Center in the hospital he served. He went to the room of a young couple who had just lost a much-wanted child in their seventh month of pregnancy, and both were weeping profusely. He brought the usual elements used in that hospital for ministry in such settings, including a seashell and small bowl of water used to baptize pre-term children. A nurse handed him the body of the baby, and he began the prayer suggested for these circumstances. As he picked up the shell to scoop water onto the baby's head, he took in the grief of these parents fully. He put down the seashell and, after asking their permission, touched his fingertip to the tears on each parent's cheek, then used those tears to baptize the baby. Like this chaplain, you can offer the best care when you are fully present to others and to God in your body, mind, heart, words, actions, and spirit.

Awareness at the End of Life

One ongoing question in end-of-life care is this: when a person is very near death, perhaps unconscious, how aware are they of what is happening around them? Can they hear people talking or understand what is being said?

Most experienced end-of-life caregivers suggest "yes, they do." For example, I was called to be with a family whose father was actively dying. He had been comatose and unresponsive since the day before, and they knew the end was very near. I invited the family to gather around the bed and took one of the man's hands in mine as I prayed, asking God for comfort and reassurance for him and for his family as he made the journey Home. As I said "Amen," the man firmly and deliberately squeezed my hand. I am certain that whether or not he understood the words I had said, he knew he was being prayed for, and that was important to him.

So many similar experiences have occurred in my ministry and in those of colleagues that it seems clear that at some level even those very near death are aware of what is said and done. Prayers and the administration of sacraments (if appropriate) should assume the dying person knows or senses what is happening, and last interactions with the dying need to be especially sensitive and compassionate.

Engaging Loved Ones

One important pastoral task is to help the dying persons and their loved ones say "good-bye" to one another. With extended illnesses, this hopefully has happened over the course of the person's final days. In the case of accidents or other sudden life-threatening situations, this will not have happened.

If the dying person is conscious, you can encourage her and her family to share their final thoughts and feelings. Melanie, a hospice chaplain, explicitly asks both the dying person and his or her family members, "Is there anything incomplete for you? Anyone who needs to forgive you? Anyone you need to forgive? Anyone you need reconciliation with?"[26] Byock's "Four Things" can shape this process. The point is to help persons say what they most need to one another.

If the dying person is unconscious, since he is likely aware at some level of what is happening, you can encourage his family to express their love, gratitude, or whatever is appropriate to him, trusting that he will hear it. Often what a dying person most needs is permission and blessing to move on; helping loved ones provide that will be good for everyone.

You may also wish to invite loved ones into a ritual, including praying for the dying person. Having them gather around the bed, holding hands if they are comfortable doing so, and praying with and for them can be very powerful. Or inviting them to sing a favorite hymn together as the person is dying can be a lovely way to help "sing them home."

Care for the Newly Bereaved

As you saw in the stories that begin this chapter, loved ones' responses to the fact of recent death are varied. Like Jacob in the biblical story or the father in the E.R., they may be torn by anger, outrage, or grief. Like Pearl's family, they may be more accepting and more at peace with what is happening. Like Pete's family, they may be so distraught they are unable to be there at the time of death. Every person and every family will respond in their own way to the sharp grief of someone's passing. How can you help?

First Contact

It is often the case that you will be called by a family member when someone has died rather than you yourself being there at the moment of death. If possible, take a moment to center yourself — to pray, to notice your own feelings, to breathe through any anxiety you may have.

Next, express your care and concern for the person calling. You may feel that saying "I'm so sorry" doesn't help much, but it does. That person is hurting and needs to know that others care.

Then you can gather some information. When did the person die? Sometimes people won't call you for a day or two after the death, depending on your role and relationship with them. If the death occurred in the past hour or two, where is the family now, e.g., at home, at the hospital, at the nursing home? Are there other people with the person who has called you to help support them? Finally, would they like you to come then, or wait until later?

Acknowledging the Death

If you are welcome to join the family, do so. Whether you go to their home or meet them at the hospital, if the body of the person who has died is still there, acknowledge that person's presence and passing. Sometimes simply saying something to the deceased like, "George, I am really going to miss you," is very comforting for the bereaved, even if it feels a little strange to you. If they are open to prayer, you might lightly touch the shoulder of the deceased as you pray, including him or her in the prayer-circle. If your tradition includes anointing the body, this is a helpful reminder of God's care and blessing.

Next Steps

If you are not their regular pastor, offer to contact him or her. Stay with them until their pastor arrives, if possible.

Whether they are at home, in the hospital, or at another care facility, make sure that everyone has time to say their good-byes. At the hospital, if family were waiting somewhere other than the patient's room, offer to escort them to see their loved one. Encourage and help them do what they need to do to acknowledge the person's death. When they are ready, alert hospital or mortuary staff, then escort the family to another area of the house (perhaps the backyard) or to the hospital or care facility family room while the body is removed.

Sitting and Listening

If the death has just occurred, bereaved people may simply need you to sit with them. They may still be in shock, unable to think or plan yet. Being able to sit calmly in silence can be a great gift. This can be a deeply sacred time. You don't need to do or say anything other than be there, representing the love of God and showing your own care. Families will do and say what they need to, usually with little assistance from you. They may need to weep for a while or tell stories or drink coffee or talk with each other as if you weren't there. Whatever happens, your quiet faithful presence will be reassuring and comforting.

As is always true with pastoral conversations, when they are ready to talk, simply follow their lead. It is not helpful to try to cheer them up or reassure them that all will be well — at that moment, things are very much not well. Help them tell their stories. They may need to review past months if the death has been long in coming or rehearse over and over tragic events that have suddenly occurred. As they speak, they may alternate between lamenting and laughter. Listen for what was important to them about this person, and listen for what they need pastorally.

Other Tasks

As they mention contacting other family and friends, you may ask if they want help with that. Most families do not but may appreciate your contacting other church or community members to whom they are particularly close. It is empowering for them to make as many of these calls as they can, but in the case of sudden unexpected death, they may be too much in shock to do so. In such cases, your offer to make calls may be a welcome help.

Some families will want to immediately start making funeral plans. You will learn to discern this, but usually the hours immediately following a death are not a good time to do that. Instead, call them later that day or the next day, after they have had some time to be with what is happening and talk with others affected by the death. It takes time for the reality of a death to sink in and for the bereaved to begin to shift gears emotionally and mentally to what needs to be done next. Try not to let your anxiety or need to "do something" for them impel you to start asking them questions related to funeral planning too soon.

If you have any discussion about the funeral at the time of death, it is enough to reassure them that you know exactly what needs to be done. Many people assume they need to know how to plan a funeral, and since few have ever done that, they will be frightened and anxious because they don't know what to do. A calm reminder that you have done this before will offer them relief and comfort.

Try not to leave a bereaved person alone when you must depart. Some very elderly people may not have family close at hand or many surviving friends, so helping find someone to be with them is wise. Remember, they are almost certainly disoriented and confused, and perhaps exhausted as well, especially if the death has been a long time coming. At this time, they need concrete physical and emotional care from others.

Sudden Death

Most of this chapter addresses situations where death is impending, or is not totally unexpected. But what happens if it is not? For example, when a mother miscarries a much-wanted child? Or a woman finds her life-partner dead in the bathtub? Or the police notify a family that a loved one has been murdered?

Each of these sudden deaths will affect survivors differently but all in ways that necessitate special kinds of pastoral care. We will briefly consider each situation.

In the past, it was not uncommon to dismiss *pre-term losses* as "not real deaths," since the child was never born. To the joyful and excited parents-to-be, however, the loss may be as real and as painful if it occurs three months into a pregnancy as if it occurs after the birth. Miscarriages and stillbirths are often agonizing to expectant parents, and they need very tender care in their grief.

Many birth centers have special chaplains on call, and special procedures for supporting the grieving parents. In a hospital I served, for example, we always offered to baptize the pre-term child[27] using a special ritual developed by the pastoral care department. We encouraged parents to hold their baby, to name their child, to talk about their plans and dreams for her or him, and to say good-bye.

The *unexpected death of an older person* is distressing in different ways. Finding one's spouse dead in the bathroom, or not having waked up from an afternoon nap, is deeply traumatic. People are overwhelmed mentally and emotionally and may retreat into denial or shock. There is a sense of unreality that this has happened. Even when people think to call 911, they may be confused or surprised when the response team arrives. They will often need to tell the story of the discovery and what happened next over and over in an attempt to make it real for themselves. Going to them promptly (if they permit it) is important, and patient pastoral support afterward will be invaluable.

If you are a hospital chaplain, victim's advocate, social services worker, or police chaplain, you will almost certainly be faced with persons bereaved by *murder*. This may also occur to parish pastors as will the need to respond when there are deaths by *suicide*.

In these cases, bereaved persons also often suffer from a sense of unreality, sometimes combined with rage — toward the person who has died, toward the assailant, even toward first responders, including ministers. They will be barraged by professionals reacting to a crisis situation often so focused on their work that they are unable to respond to the needs of the bereaved. At this time of intense pain, they will be asked to deal with unfamiliar events and possibilities. They may be required to respond to lengthy questioning by police or medical staff.

Again, your presence may be crucial to help ground and support them. You may be able to use your position to obtain information that is not being provided to family, and to liaison between family and public safety or medical professionals. In traumatic situations like these, you may also be able to help connect them with specially trained professionals who can help them with what has happened in ways you cannot.

Chapter Eight

Care for the Bereaved: The Remembrance Service

The archers shot King Josiah; and the king said to his servants, "Take me away, for I am badly wounded." So his servants took him out of the chariot and carried him in his second chariot and brought him to Jerusalem. There he died, and was buried in the tombs of his ancestors. All Judah and Jerusalem mourned for Josiah. Jeremiah also uttered a lament for Josiah, and all the singing men and singing women have spoken of Josiah in their laments to this day. They made these a custom in Israel; they are recorded in the Laments. — 2 Chronicles 35:23–25

Uttering Laments

Early in my ministry, a member of my church died after a long struggle with chronic illness. His wife was also a church member, and their son lived in our city. An adult daughter, whom I'd never heard mentioned before the man died, lived across the country.

Not knowing any better, I planned his service with the wife and son, who both reassured me that the daughter would be fine with whatever we decided. The day of the service, a few minutes before it began, she arrived, and we were introduced. It was clear that she was very upset and angry. She asked if she could say a few words during the service, and I consented.

After her brother offered a warm and glowing tribute to their father, she stood and stiffly walked to the lectern. She began a diatribe against her father, mother, and brother, which there was

99

no way gracefully to stop. Everyone there was clearly shocked and appalled, including me. When she finished speaking, she stormed out of the church. I have never forgotten how distressing this must have been for the whole family, including the daughter herself. Colleagues have since shared similar stories. We have all learned the importance of trying to include every member of a family in planning services, no matter how distant.

Why Have a Service?

A growing trend in our society is to have no funeral service.[28] Family members increasingly ask mortuaries (or occasionally pastors) to "dispose of" the body or cremains for them, often without a family member even being present.

However, from a pastoral care perspective, having a service of some kind is vitally important. Emotionally, it helps the family begin to accept the reality of the death, it may begin repairing damaged relationships, and it offers a consoling reminder of the care of others. Theologically, it helps them find meaning in their loss, reassurance that they are not alone, comfort from the promise of God's care for them and their loved one, and, in the Christian faith, the assurance of eternal life. More broadly, it helps other members of the community with their grief, whether they are friends of the deceased, part of the larger faith family, or professional caregivers who helped care for the deceased.

If family members resist the idea of having a service, you might gently explore their reasons. They may be worried because they are unfamiliar with church services or because they have had bad experiences at funerals they have attended. They may be afraid that family secrets will come to light or anxious about the costs of a service. While it is not the pastor's job to coerce or force anyone to have a service they genuinely do not want, reminders of your care, the community's, and God's may help them make a decision they will be glad about long term.

Pastoral Approaches

Every pastor develops her or his own approach to funeral planning and celebration. Many factors, including your particular faith tradition, shape the service. Even within a specified format, each pastor will insert his or her own character into the service.

Every pastor prepares differently. Some use a check-list to cover all facets of the service and write their homilies out in full. Other pastors prefer to leave many service details open and to create their message during the service itself. Others have a set of funeral homilies they rotate between services, modifying details, depending on circumstances. Personally I believe this last practice disrespects mourners' needs, but it seems to work for some ministers and grieving families.

You will prayerfully discern what is most helpful to those you serve and how God is calling you to prepare and lead these services. That said, the rest of this chapter will consider some basic guidelines helpful in planning and celebrating these occasions.

Meeting with the Family

Where and When

The family will usually be ready to meet to discuss the service a day or two after the death. They may still be in shock, have not yet accepted the reality of their loss, be exhausted from caregiving, or be struggling with other emotional and cognitive issues that make planning anything, especially an event this important, difficult. They will be grateful to learn that you know what is needed and will help them through what needs to be done.

You may meet with the family at their home, at your office, or at the mortuary, depending on their preference. If they are church members, they may enjoy being in a familiar place with good memories. If they are very tired, they may find it easier to have you come to them. Sharing a cup of tea in their kitchen can be relaxing and connectional at a very difficult time.

Some grievers will want to keep the "business" side of the service — their planning with the mortuary — private, while others
will find your participation there helpful. In situations where the
bereaved person has no nearby family or support network, she
may appreciate the comfort of your presence as she struggles
with unfamiliar and painful tasks like deciding about cremation
or selecting a casket.

Whether you accompany them or not, you can remind them
that the mortuary staff is part of their care team too. Most mortuary personnel are deeply compassionate people whose work with
the bereaved is a ministry for them. They can help the bereaved
with practical issues like obtaining death certificates, information
about veterans' benefits, insurance regulations, and more.[29]

Who's Who

Families today can be complicated, especially with separations,
remarriages, and so forth. Most of the time, you will know who
the primary bereaved person is. For example, with couples, it is
usually the current spouse.[30] For elderly single adults, it will often
be an adult child. This is the person you will contact regarding
service planning and whose needs are generally uppermost in your
caregiving. If this is not clear, you will need to find out that person's name, their relationship to the deceased, and their contact
information.

If a family is large, and you don't know the extended family
members, you may make a list of who is who. If the family uses
nicknames (especially for the deceased) be sure you have noted
that "J.D." and "John" are the same person, but that "Cammy"
and "Camilla" are not. You may want to refer back to your list
later while planning your homily or if you need to ask follow-up
questions.

Clarify each person's relationship to the deceased. It is hurtful
to family if you refer to "Karen" as the "grand-daughter" when she
is the daughter, or to refer to family members by wrong names. It
may feel a little impersonal to be constructing a family tree as you

meet with grieving people, but this often turns into a wonderful opportunity for storytelling.

Family Dynamics

Funerals and funeral planning may bring out the best or the worst in people. If the family is healthy, it will often provide an opportunity for them to express their love and to offer one another support and hope. If they are not (and in most families there are at least some old unresolved conflicts), old pain, anger, or tension may arise as you meet with them. Or it may come out "sideways" at the service, as happened in the family whose story began this chapter.

Family members are sometimes troubled in other ways that affect their interactions. Some members struggle with mental illnesses or with addictions. These trials may have been lifelong concerns both for that member and the family, or may have been kept from others and emerge in the stress of their loss.

Sometimes there are deep and upsetting family secrets. A parent may have abused the children. A spouse or partner may have been violent. The deceased may have been involved in illegal activities or died in questionable circumstances. Some families still find deaths from cancer or from AIDS shameful.

In such cases, long-suppressed pain can flare up in the face of loss and of family interactions that may occur for the first time in many years. The pastoral task is to be attentive to emotional patterns and dynamics and to mediate and moderate as needed.

Funerals for People You Don't Know

Depending on your area of ministry, you may be asked to lead funerals for people you don't know. For example, you may be new in the parish you serve when a longtime church member (whom you have not yet met) dies. Or you will receive calls from adult children whose recently deceased parents were members of the church many years before. Or you may be asked to perform services for relatives of church members. And chaplains, especially those in hospice work, may have only the briefest acquaintance with persons they are asked to bury.

In these cases, it is especially helpful to have a checklist or a set of questions to guide your conversation and the family's decision-making. Whether meeting in person or over the phone, you can invite them to tell you about the deceased and what they want to honor and celebrate about that person's life. In these situations, most families deeply appreciate your willingness to create a meaningful service, and you may be surprised at how easily you move into a pastoral relationship with them.

Elements of the Service

Decisions about the shape and nature of the service will be determined by the faith tradition of the presiding minister, that of the deceased (if different), and that of the family members. Your denomination will have certain stipulations about what must or may be included in a funeral. For example, some denominations allow great latitude in who may lead the service, which Scripture passages may be used, and how music is used. Others are more restrictive about specifics of the liturgy and about leadership.

Learn the expectations of your tradition, so you can work within them to bless both the life you are celebrating and the grief of those left behind. Families often don't understand why things should be done in a certain way (e.g., why an open casket or closed casket is the usual custom) especially if they come from a different faith background (or from none). Your explanation of why certain practices are observed will help them engage more meaningfully in the service.

If you are leading a service for a deceased person from a tradition different from yours, your pastoral challenge will be to offer a service that respects both their tradition and yours. If allowed, you can incorporate elements of their tradition into the service. For example, a member of my congregation was both a practicing Quaker and a member of the UCC. At her service, we followed the outline of the UCC liturgy and included elements of a Quaker service as well. This was deeply meaningful to her family and to other mourners.

It may happen that a family is uncomfortable including liturgical or faith language that is an integral part of your tradition. For example, they might say, "We don't believe in that resurrection stuff and don't want it in the service." In such cases, you can either agree to do what they request or gracefully offer to help them find another officiant who can offer the kind of service they want.

Theological Considerations

First and foremost, these services are services of worship. They are gifts we offer primarily to God, not primarily to mourners (although that is one component). Above all, they are not a glorification of the deceased, but a celebration and thanksgiving to the God with whom that person now rests and who is present to comfort and sustain the mourners.

A eulogy is about the person who has died. It is usually an extension of the information that appeared in the obituary. In contrast, a homily or sermon is about God. Your job, as spiritual leader, is to help mourners make the connections between that person's life, their own feelings of loss, and the continuing care of the God who loves and holds them.

That said, it is important to reflect specifically on the one you are remembering so that mourners know whose life it is you are celebrating. An authentic and meaningful message will lift up the joys and sorrows that mourners have shared, describe the good qualities of and happy memories shared with the deceased, and be directed primarily to the family and their needs. Generally, families will receive the most satisfaction and consolation from a service that offers a balance between remembrances of their loved one, music that speaks to their needs, and Scripture, prayers, and words of faith that remind them of God's care for their loved one and themselves.

Practical Considerations

Basic considerations include where and when the service will be. If you are a parish pastor, it will usually be in the church, though not always. Some families will request a service at the mortuary (especially if many attending are likely to be non-church people), at the graveside, or occasionally at the family's home. If you minister in another setting, it may be in a hospital or hospice chapel, or elsewhere.

The date set for the service often depends on how geographically widespread the family is. It is increasingly common not to have the service within the week of the death, but sometimes much later, when it is more convenient for family to travel and gather. Once the date of service has been determined, the time of day of the celebration will depend largely on the family's preference, on availability of the facility where the service will be held, and if a graveside service, on the hours the cemetery is open and able to inter bodies or cremains.

Another consideration is whether the deceased's body is to be buried or cremated. Hopefully, the deceased will have made his or her wishes clear before death occurs. If not, you may have extensive opportunities for pastoral care as family members struggle with this decision. For many, it is based on spiritual and emotional considerations, and sorting these out, especially when family members come from different perspectives, can be challenging.

One related issue for the service is whether there will be a casket (which may be open or closed) or an urn containing cremains present at the service. Some traditions permit any of these options, and some do not. You will help families reflect on their preferences and what is possible in this regard.

A final consideration is whether there will be a service at the cemetery following the primary worship service elsewhere. For burials, there is usually a second brief service called a committal service at the cemetery following the church service. When cremation has occurred, interment may occur sometime later. The family may want to keep the urn for a while before scattering the "ashes" at a special location or at a later gathering of the extended family for interment, an occasion at which you may offer to preside.

Music

Music has become a trickier issue for ministers than in times past, when most denominations had a set of "funeral hymns" that were always sung at services. Today families may request very different kinds of music. It will be your job to gently educate them about music appropriate for these occasions, guided both by their needs and by the rubrics of your denomination.

If the deceased was a church member, you might ask whether that person had favorite hymns. If so, which of those would also bring hope and comfort to the family? Do family members have favorite hymns? If the person (or mourners) had other favorite music, how could that be made a relevant part of the service?

Families also have preferences about singing during the service. Some will love the comfort of singing hymns together as a community, while others are uncomfortable with this. Some will ask to play recorded music, which your worship setting may or may not permit or be able to provide.

Some family members may also wish to play or sing during the service. In the moment, this can turn out to be far more difficult than they expected, and they may find themselves unable to continue. Discuss this honestly beforehand. If they feel able to do this, and it means a lot to them to do so, it can be deeply healing for them.

Readings

Since this is a worship service, you will probably include Scripture readings. If family members mention favorite passages, you may want to include those in the service. If you do, it is helpful during the service to mention briefly why certain readings were selected; for example, "This was one of Ruben's favorite passages, and it brought him a lot of comfort during his illness."

Simply asking families "what Scripture readings would you like?" can put them in an awkward situation. People from other faith traditions, or who are non-churchgoers, may be embarrassed that they are unfamiliar with the Bible. Even longtime church-goers are in a state of great emotional stress, and nothing may readily come to mind.

If they don't have specific ideas, you can offer suggestions. As the homilist, you may want to include readings relevant to your sermon. If you have already thought about this, you could mention texts that came to mind as you thought about the deceased. If not, there are many beloved Scripture passages with which many people are familiar and will find comforting. Your denomination's Book of Worship will also list suggestions.

Some family members may also want to include other readings, like favorite poems or other texts that were meaningful to the deceased or to them. Letters they have written to their loved one during the dying process may be important to read aloud as a way of sharing their feelings with the community. In one deeply touching service, a young teen granddaughter read a prayer she had written for her dying grandfather, which had been framed and placed at his bedside. In my experience, these are usually very appropriate and very meaningful to mourners.

If such readings are included, and especially if family want to be the readers or to speak in other ways, it is wise to decide which person will speak first. He or she can then be encouraged to model for those who will follow the kind of remarks and presentation style that are appropriate.

In addition, you may request that speakers provide you with a written copy of what they plan to read or say before the service. Then, if they discover they are unable to read or break down while speaking you can gracefully step in and share the words for them.

Participants

Sometimes family will want a former pastor to perform the service, especially if they have a long relationship with her or him. Or they will want another pastor to preach the homily, since "you're new and didn't really know the deceased." (The first two years of your ministry in a new location are likely to be the most challenging in this respect.) You may be disappointed or feel resentful about this, especially if you have been providing care for the family. To the degree possible, honor their needs first.

Ethically, most denominations prohibit former pastors from accepting such invitations. This is because you are now the person's pastor and can best help mourners through all their grief work if you also work with them on service preparation and celebration. If another pastor presides, while he or she may be there for the service, you are the one who will do the long-term bereavement care. It can be a delicate matter, but usually with a thoughtful explanation from you, families will understand, and welcome your ministry to them.

Sometimes family will request a time in the service when their friends may come forward and speak. While this seems to be a welcoming way to support others' grief, it is in fact usually not a helpful practice. Spontaneous speakers may tell stories that are inappropriate or distressing to the primary mourners. Others seize the opportunity as a chance to "preach" and may do so inappropriately. Speakers may talk far longer than is comfortable for the family and other mourners. If a family requests this, you may suggest that instead of people speaking during the service, they share their stories about the deceased during the post-service meal or other informal gathering.

If the deceased belonged to an organization like the Masons or Eastern Star, a representative from that group may wish to recognize the deceased by participating in the service. Many such organizations have prescribed rituals for these occasions and ask to perform them either in the context of the service or during the interment. Sometimes the theological understandings contained in such ceremonies will be congruent with those of your faith tradition. Sometimes they will not. If you can determine beforehand what participants wish to say and do, you can decide if and how their ritual might be integrated into the service. Often it is more appropriate to arrange for such observances to be cele-brated at a different time from the funeral or after the funeral is completed.

Pastorally, if the deceased has been dedicated to the organiza-tion, or if it plays a significant role in your community, it may be an important part of the grieving and healing processes to allow these rituals to be included. Consultation with other pastors in your community, careful attention to the needs of the bereaved, and your prayerful consideration will help you decide how to handle these issues.

Symbols

It can be deeply meaningful to display mementos that were sig-nificant to the deceased in the service itself. I have celebrated services where we variously displayed pictures drawn by grand-children, a plastic singing fish, and a retired railroad engineer's cap and badge. If your tradition permits, photos of the deceased (and family) might be placed in a prominent location. This can also be done with other special objects like recognitions of the person's military service, vocation, or avocations, like quilts or other artistic work. Whether or not these appear in the sanctuary space, families usually find it very healing to put together photo displays and place them wherever there will be a gathering after the service. Viewing old pictures can spark conversations, evoke old memories of happy times, and help people support one another who may otherwise find it difficult to know what to say.

Story Telling

After discussing relevant service details, you will move to the most important part of the meeting — sharing stories. Some families do this spontaneously, while others need encouragement. Sometimes a simple "tell me about Anne" will be all that it takes. Other times, specific questions like "How did you two meet?" or "What is the funniest thing you remember about your mom?" can help people begin reflecting aloud. Usually, as people begin to share, one story will beget another as they fondly argue about which one was the best family vacation they ever had or what they remember about growing up on the farm together.

As stories are told, there may be tears as well as laughter. Old pain may resurface, as they struggle with disappointments about relationships with the deceased. New pain may emerge as old family secrets are shared for the first time. New joy may be found as old misunderstandings are cleared away. Whatever the nature of the conversation, the healing process can begin, as mourners begin to acknowledge the reality of their loss, renegotiate their relationships (since their roles will have changed with the loss of their loved one), and share their care for one another. As you listen with the ears of your heart, you may notice that themes emerge that you will want to incorporate into your sermon or homily.

The Message

As a rule, it is not so much what you say in the homily as how you say it and how you are present with the family that matters most. Even so, you will want to construct your message with care.

In most traditions, part of the pastoral charge is to celebrate the life of the deceased. You might do this through describing that person's good qualities as they have been conveyed by family, their accomplishments, their contributions to the community and world, their faith life, and whatever else is appropriate. If you take the time to listen well and to lift up what grievers most want celebrated, they will feel heard and their loved one acknowledged with grace and integrity.

Your task is also to honor the living. Realistically speaking, most people are not saints and have done wrong things or hurt those who love them. If everyone knows that this person abused his spouse or neglected her children or struggled with an addiction, failing to acknowledge that in some (even if very indirect) way can undermine the sincerity of everything else you have to say. If the person committed suicide or was murdered, there are additional levels of anger, grief, and loss for grievers beyond those faced by those who lose loved ones to natural causes. The challenge is how to acknowledge those difficult realities in a way that is respectful and has integrity regarding both the deceased and those who mourn.

One pastor celebrated the funeral of a man whose wife was a member of his congregation, though the deceased was not. As the pastor met with her and her adult children to plan the service, their anger and anguish were apparent. They revealed that he had repeatedly abused all of them. They couldn't bear the thought that in the funeral he would be lauded and their pain would go unacknowledged. The pastor very prayerfully and carefully constructed a message that acknowledged both the man's "lights" and his "shadows." It was deeply healing for both the family and the community.

Most important, your pastoral task is to lift up the message of faith. In part, you do that by celebrating the deceased as a beloved child of God. A thoughtful homily will tie together faith beliefs with the life of both the dead and the living. Equally important, whether mourners are regular church-goers or not, most will find great solace in being reminded of the loving and eternal care of God for their loved one and themselves.

Finally, there may be nothing harder than officiating at the service of a child or teenager. As described later, bereaved parents have very special pastoral needs, and it is almost impossible to "celebrate" their child's life when they are filled with so much pain at their loss. What, then, can you say? Very often it is most comforting to acknowledge that there is nothing to say that will take away their pain, and that when deaths like these occur, it is very hard to understand why. It is also helpful to celebrate the good things they remember about their child, and the joy she or he brought to others' lives. Remember, it is not your words, so much as your presence, both as supporter and as a representative of the God who cares about them, that will matter most.

Occasions of Care

Before the Service

In addition to the care you extend while planning the service, two other possibilities may occur for offering care. As noted above, one is that of visiting the funeral home with the primary grievers, as they make arrangements for their loved one's final disposition. In some communities, it is expected the pastor will do this. In others, grievers will indicate whether or not your presence is welcome.

A second opportunity occurs in communities that have a time of visitation (also called a "viewing" or "wake") before the service. Typically, this will occur at the funeral home, often a day in advance of the funeral, and usually with the body of the deceased present. The purpose is for mourners to pay their respects to the dead and to greet and console the family. Some faith communities also offer a brief worship service in conjunction with the viewing.

On such occasions, the pastor's presence is usually welcomed and appreciated. The immediate family may welcome a prayer before others arrive or after they leave. Your denominational tradition and that of your community will help you discern if and how to participate in these events.

Day of the Service

Before the service, it is calming to gather the family in a private space where they don't have to interact with others, such as your office or the church library. Some may wish to greet others as they arrive, but many will be so exhausted or emotional that it is simply too difficult to do so. Follow their lead in where they wish to be and how they wish to be together.

You will serve the family best in this interval by ensuring that other details are taken care of, and you will serve other mourners by being available near the sanctuary to greet people as they arrive. Just before the service begins, you may gather with the family, check on any final concerns they may have, and offer a prayer focused on their pastoral needs that day.

While leading the service, your calm, centered, faithful presence will reassure and comfort them. Telling their loved one's story and their own will honor all of their lives and their relationships. Tying their story to God's story will give them hope and help them move into the future.

Following the service, you will escort them out. Again, denominations have different practices, depending on whether there is a casket or not, whether celebrants and family typically precede or follow the casket, and so forth. Your tradition's Book of Worship will usually offer guidance. Once the family is out of the sanctuary, it is supportive to escort them to the social hall, or wherever the after-service gathering is to occur.

If no gathering is planned, and you are proceeding immediately to the cemetery, you may wish to drive yourself, or to ride in the hearse. Generally, pastors do not travel with family members. They need some time to recompose themselves before the interment.

A few days after the service you will want to make a follow-up phone call and perhaps extend further bereavement care. That is the subject of the next chapter.

Chapter Nine

Care for the Bereaved:
After the Service Is Over

Blessed are those who mourn, for they will be comforted.
—Matthew 5:4

Those Who Mourn

Alma and Ralph were married for fifty-eight years when Ralph developed congestive heart failure and died. A few days after the funeral, Alma began to experience severe chest-pains. A check-up revealed normal heart function, but the pains continued, along with backaches. She also shared with her pastor that she wasn't sleeping much and had lost about ten pounds since she "just wasn't hungry."

Terry and Kim had three children and were expecting a fourth when their youngest child, four-year-old Andy, developed leukemia. They gathered their resources, determined to explore every possible treatment. They took turns sitting at Andy's bed-side as he moaned in pain from treatments or chafed at not being able to get out of bed and play. They and their church family prayed for his recovery. Despite their care, the disease finally took Andy's life. As his funeral ended, they both wondered if their lives would ever be the same again.

Anna and Chris had been together for twenty-four years when Chris developed breast-cancer. In spite of extensive treatment, she died eighteen months after diagnosis. Because she and Anna had been very private about their relationship, many of their acquaintances assumed they were simply longtime friends. Thus, while people were supportive of Anna in her loss, it was a different kind of support than they would have offered to a grieving widow.

Sam was seven when his dad got really sick. He couldn't play ball with Sam anymore or go to work. Sam felt mad a lot, and confused. He wondered if it was his fault his dad was sick. When his dad died, he was scared about whether his mom could take care of him and his sister. At night, he would look up at the sky and pray that his dad would come back. Deborah, his teenage sister, said that was dumb, that Daddy had gone to heaven, and was never coming back.

Bereavement

The word "bereaved" means "robbed of." Those who are bereaved have been robbed of many things: a cherished companion, a beloved parent, shared love, activities enjoyed together, hopes and dreams, feelings of safety, and more. They may feel angry, wronged, despairing, and helpless. The range of emotions, physical effects, cognitive disturbances, and spiritual struggles the bereaved experience — that complex we call "grief" — may be so overwhelming that caregivers may wonder, "Can I really help someone through this?" The good news is, yes, with God's help, you can.

Grief is a process. It occurs through time, and takes time. It has no fixed duration, so there is no point in time at which grievers should be "finished" or past their grief. It comes and goes, sometimes triggered by surprising causes.

Grief also involves work. Erich Lindemann, who originated this idea, described what grievers must do to engage with their feelings and so "work through" their grief and toward a life that is again rich and meaningful.[31] You will discover that many grievers simply want to "get on with life," rather than doing the work of grieving. While this is natural, it is not constructive in the long run.

Finally, as described earlier, grief is multidimensional. As Alma's example illustrates, grief is not "just" a feeling, but affects every level of the bereaved person's life and functioning. Their bodies may ache, hunger, be exhausted. Their minds may wander or have trouble discerning between what is real and what is not. Their hearts may be wrenched with the pain of what they have lost or never had. Their spirits struggle to make sense of their loss, and come to grips with a radically changed world.

Losing a Life-Companion

Despite increasingly grim statistics on marriage failures, for most people it is still the long-term relationship model of choice. When couples speak their vows, they do so with high hopes and great expectations for their future together.

This is also true for couples who, for legal or other reasons, do not marry. Gay and lesbian couples or heterosexual couples who cohabit long term seek and find the same joys and challenges in their relationships that married couples do.

All long-term committed relationships, at their best, offer a particular identity, financial security, emotional safety, sexual fulfillment, a helpmate with basic life tasks, a co-parent if children are included in the relationship, and more. Lifelong companions are friends, lovers, advisors, links to extended family, and lifetime partners. Thus, the loss of a life-partner entails uncountable losses beyond that of the person herself or himself and may require more adjustment than does any other life event.[32]

Widows and Widowers

Most studies of bereavement have focused on widows and widowers. These studies reveal that women and men experience spousal loss very differently and that the life-period in which a spouse is lost also affects the grieving process.

Widows often feel abandoned, sometimes with a deep sense of injustice. For example, one widow commented, "It's not fair. We both just retired, and we were supposed to be able to enjoy our golden years together." They are also likely to be at greater risk financially and worry more about security for themselves and for their children. They are more likely to be excluded from social gatherings. If they wish to begin a new relationship, there are fewer eligible men to date (especially as they grow older) and fewer acceptable ways to meet those singles.

Emotionally, women are more likely to feel anger and deep sadness at their loss. They are more likely to express their emotions, to feel their way through their grief process, and to experience complicated grief. Short-term they tend to cope fairly effectively with their loss, but long-term they are much more likely to have severe physical or emotional problems "and their long-term adjustment tends to be less satisfactory."[33]

Widowers are more likely to feel guilt or remorse, especially for not having taken better care of their wives. For example, a widower lamented, "I wish I had paid more attention when she said she was having headaches. Maybe if I'd made her go see the doctor, she'd be okay now." While men of all ages are less likely to be at financial risk in these situations, many have more problems coping with practical tasks like cooking and housekeeping. They also have more difficulty than widows when coping with the responsibilities of being a single parent.

Social stereotypes still discourage men from expressing feelings of grief, leading men to be more prone to try to think their way through their grief work. They are more likely to return to their paid jobs quickly, to neglect their own physical needs, to rely on alcohol or other drugs to assuage their pain, and to commit suicide. Men are at greatest risk in the period immediately following their loss. If they negotiate that time successfully, they typically begin to date again much sooner than widows do, are able to find new partners more easily, and are more likely to remarry.

Other Committed Relationships

Every year the percentage of heterosexual couples living together without being married rises dramatically. This relational style includes both young and older persons. Although unmarried couples are less likely to have children than are married couples, many do become (or are) parents and in most other ways are very similar to married partners. The major difference is that unmarried couples do not enjoy the same legal, social, and religious supports that accrue to married couples.

This is especially true for homosexual couples. Only a handful of states as of this writing have extended legal protections through domestic partnership laws or legal marriage to lesbian and gay couples. This means that basic rights enjoyed by non-gay couples, such as hospital visitation, health benefits, leave to care for a sick companion, bereavement leave, and inheritance rights are not available to most gay or lesbian life-partners. Thus, as for Chris at this chapter's beginning, during the most frightening and difficult times in their lives, the social supports that sustain others are not available. In fact, their pain and grief may be exacerbated by those who do not understand or "approve of" their relationship. This often leads to unrecognized or unsanctioned grief, with all its complications.

Whether straight or gay, when persons in an unmarried committed relationship lose their life-companion, they experience the same deep grief and varied losses as do persons who were legally married. And they often experience their pain and loss without the care and support of their own or their companion's extended family, empathetic friends, or a compassionate faith community.

These bereaved may be denied permission to express their grief publicly. They may be deliberately excluded from participation in funeral arrangements and services by other family members. And they seldom receive time off from work to grieve or to be with and support their children.

At the same time, they are faced with the same practical concerns and difficulties with regard to child-care, home management, and work requirements that face all bereaved people. They may also be forced to struggle with an array of legal difficulties related to property ownership and other inheritance matters. Finally, they too face the challenges of developing new relationships and new commitments. Clearly, it is crucial for caregivers to be aware of both the usual and the special circumstances these persons face and to devote suitable time and attention to their needs.

Life-Period of Loss

Persons at different points in their long-term relationships face different developmental tasks and emotional issues. For example, newly married couples are mostly concerned with forming their own family system, which is both distinct from and connected to their families of origin. Their primary emotional focus is on each other and on negotiating their newly discovered similarities and differences as they also face career and emerging family challenges. In contrast, middle-aged couples often have fewer concerns about establishing careers or financial security, but may be negotiating both the changing needs of their young adult children and those of their aging parents. Elderly couples have experienced the varied gifts and challenges of very long-term relationships, coupled with the new physical and financial concerns brought by aging.

Thus, the practical assistance, emotional concerns, and spiritual needs of a bereaved person in one life-stage will be different from those of someone in a different stage. Your awareness of the dynamics of these different stages of intimate relationships, the needs those engender, and the likely available supports for persons at each stage will help you offer the most appropriate and beneficial care.

Losing a Child

Just a few generations ago, most children died in infancy or in the first years of life. Today, however, with improved health care and gentler living conditions for many, most children are expected not only to survive childhood, but to live to a ripe old age. Thus, the death of a child is usually deeply traumatic and experienced as deeply incongruent with the natural order of things.

Indeed, many describe the loss of a child as the worst possible kind of loss, and many bereaved parents describe their grief as nearly unendurable. Because of the special bonds that exist between parents and their children, the loss of a child presents distinctive concerns. As with Terry and Kim, parents who lose a child also lose "their hopes, dreams, expectations, fantasies, and wishes for that child. They have lost parts of themselves, each other, their family, and their future."[34]

Losing a child affects numerous relationships: that of parents with each other, those with their other children, and those with still others (e.g., grandparents) that exist because of the parental relationship. Each of those relationships may suffer in special ways.

The fact that parents may grieve differently from one another, combined with the depth of their grief, may make it difficult for them to support each other well at a time they most urgently need that support. They may also differ in their understandings of what has happened, be at odds over practical details like how to deal with their dead child's room or possessions, and blame each other (sometimes unconsciously) for the death of their child. Not surprisingly, divorce is common among couples who have lost a child.

Bereaved parents may also have difficulty parenting their surviving children. They may be so exhausted physically and emotionally that they have little to give to the other children. They may be so wrapped up in their own grief that they cannot see or understand the grief of their surviving children. They may try to protect those children by keeping information from them about the death, or failing to include them in service planning or other grief rituals. While often well meant, all of these behaviors make the grieving process even harder for the surviving children.

The loss of a child also affects parents' sense of identity in profound ways. Parents' perceptions of themselves as mother or father includes not just their biological relationship with their children, but many other aspects of who they are, how they function, and how they are valued in the world.

A key aspect of this identity is most parents' sense of commitment to care for and protect their children. When a child dies, parents may experience a sense of profound failure and deep guilt. In addition, feelings that the death was "wrong" or unfair may feed feelings of anger or despair. All of these may raise deep theological questions about the love, care, and justice of a God who permits (or causes) such things to happen. Thus, the loss of a child may shake the very foundations of parents' lives and belief systems. And recovery is a very long and painful process. In fact, many parents will tell you that one never fully recovers from the loss of a child.

Losing a Parent

The death of a parent is painful at every age. While it may be especially traumatic for children and teens, there are also profound loss issues for adults who lose their parents.

In Childhood

The way the young respond to the loss of a parent depends on many things, but especially on the child's (this includes adolescents) age. As you have learned, children of different ages are in different developmental periods that affect their cognitive abilities, relationships with others, and emotional responses to life events. So children understand and respond to death differently depending on where they are in the developmental process.

For example, seven-year-old Sam at the chapter's beginning responded to his father's death differently from his older sister. His feelings of guilt and responsibility and his belief in the impermanence of death are normal for a child his age, while Deborah's understandings are normal for hers.

That said, there are some similarities in the responses of children to the loss of a parent. (Losing a sibling usually raises different issues.) Like adults, children typically experience a range of feelings, especially sadness, anger, and fear. They have cognitive difficulties, including confusion and forgetfulness, and may have trouble focusing on schoolwork. Physically, they may experience eating and sleeping disruptions. Behaviorally, they may become withdrawn or act out, expressing feelings for which they have no words. Spiritually, they need the same kind of solace that adults do, knowing they can still trust in the goodness of the universe (and God), and that they are still connected to others.

Unlike adults, children are far more dependent. They require the physical and emotional care of their parents to survive, and the death of a parent may threaten that in significant ways. When death occurs, children may lose their sense of trust, security, and safety in the world, and be plagued by fears for their own well-being or that their surviving parent will die. They may develop night terrors or phobias. For children of single parents, the loss of that parent is even more frightening and will likely necessitate a major reorganization of their family structure and life, with the additional distresses that will bring.

Because children are often not told what is happening when a parent is dying, they are deprived of the chance to express their love for that person, to say good-bye, and to do some helpful anticipatory grieving. Thus, they may experience the death both as a shock and as a betrayal, especially if they have been told, "It's okay, Mommy is going to be just fine." It is far more helpful, both before an impending death and after a death occurs, to be truthful with children, offering them age-appropriate explanations, and encouraging them to openly and honestly express their feelings.

It is also important to include them in mourning observances such as viewings and funerals, at the child's discretion. While children should not be forced to participate in such grief rituals, they should be given a choice about whether they wish to do so, and their choice should be respected.

In Adulthood

In the normal cycle of life, adults can expect to lose their parents. Even so, when that loss occurs, it is still painful and jarring. Whether the loss is due to physical death or to cognitive death (e.g., from dementia), losing one's parent requires the same kind of reorganizing of one's self-identity and life as any other significant loss.

Young adults who lose their parents may still be dependent on them financially and emotionally. Thus, they may share some grief characteristics seen in young bereaved children, including feelings of abandonment and fearfulness about the future. And since they have few peers who can understand what they are experiencing and thus support them appropriately, young adults who lose a parent often feel precariously alone.

While older adults may have more friends who have shared their experience of parental loss, it is no less devastating. In families where parents loved and validated their children, those bereaved may lose their main source of unconditional love and support in life. Where relationships with parents were troubled or broken, the bereaved lose the possibility that someday those relationships might be healed. The larger family structure may shift in unexpected and uncomfortable ways, as siblings take on new roles, or as their relationships come undone in the absence of the parent who held them together.

Bob was in his fifties when his elderly mother, who had had dementia and other chronic health problems for many years, died of a heart attack. Seven months later, perhaps from the loss of his life-companion, Bob's father died. As grieved as Bob had been by the loss of his mother, at the loss of his father, he described himself as feeling "like an orphan."

Becoming a member of the oldest surviving generation in the family is a life-altering event. Pastoral support can help these bereaved adult children maintain crucial human connections as they reorganize their lives and recreate their place in the world.

Losing Someone to Violence

With the rise in violent deaths in many communities today, you may be called upon to offer care in such situations. Death is painful enough when it occurs in the normal course of life events. When it occurs unexpectedly and violently (as through murder or suicide), grievers not only experience the losses described above, but additional losses as well.

They frequently feel guilt, as they review what they believe they could or should have done to prevent the death. For example, when a woman is killed by her abusive husband, family members may feel guilty for not having "made her" leave him. Or when a teenager takes her own life, her parents may feel guilty for "not having seen it coming." In such cases, only rarely could the death have been prevented, but that reality seldom prevents "if-only" thinking or relieves the guilt felt by survivors.

The bereaved may also experience deep shame. For example, the sister of a young man who killed himself said, "It was years before I could tell anyone how my brother really died. I'd say he was in an accident, rather than that he hung himself. I couldn't stand what other people would think about him or about us if they really knew the truth." Similarly, the widow of a man who was murdered by his business partner said that only her adult children knew what had really happened to their father. She was too ashamed for anyone else to know.

In these situations, the survivor's relationship with God may also be deeply affected. The God who was trusted in to keep them safe, protect the innocent, and ensure justice in the world may suddenly seem to have stopped playing by the rules or to have abandoned the one who has died and those who loved him or her. And if God has done that, how can this God be counted on now for strength and healing? Part of your task is to help them struggle with their deepest feelings and questions.

They Shall Be Comforted

Given all these needs, what are some things you can do as pastoral caregiver to help the bereaved walk this difficult part of life's path?

Making Contact

If possible, be with grievers physically. Most people in the midst of anguish need "God with skin on." A literal hand to hold or shoulder to lean on can be invaluable. If you cannot be there physically, and sometimes the many demands of ministry will make that impossible, phone calls and notes will help people remember they are being held in your thoughts and prayers and in God's care. In addition, laypeople trained to provide support in these situations can help provide a continuum of care for grievers to supplement that which you and other professionals provide.

Offering Grace

Grievers need to tell their stories, often over and over. Especially in cases of sudden death and of traumatic death, telling the story helps grievers make it real for themselves and helps them search for meaning in what has happened.

While friends and relatives want to be supportive, it may be hard for them to hear the story repeatedly, especially if they too are grieving the loss. As pastoral caregiver, you may be the one person who is willing and able to listen to what the griever needs to share. And your willingness to witness to their pain helps ground it in the larger reality of God and to connect their story with our larger faith story.

Normalizing

One of the most important things you can do for grievers is to normalize their experiences. While every person grieves differently and there is no single "normal" grief path, there are many commonalities among grievers' experiences. Caregivers can remind them that whatever they are going through, whether insomnia, physical pains, depression, panic, confusion, or something else, these are all to-be-expected parts of the grief process.

One especially disturbing experience for many grievers is difficulty concentrating. They find themselves distracted in the midst of making a sandwich or trying to do their job. They can't remember whether they took something out of the freezer for dinner, or whether they submitted the important report due to their boss. For most people, this is terrifying.

Another common experience is to see, smell, or feel their now-deceased loved one. The griever may be paying bills, look up, and see her deceased husband standing nearby. Or he may be bathing his child, and suddenly smell his deceased wife's perfume. For grievers, these kinds of perceptions are very common and absolutely real.

In situations like these, many grievers will tell you they are afraid they are "losing their minds." This, on top of everything else, can lead to feelings of panic, anxiety, or extreme fearfulness. They are walking through an unknown place, toward an uncertain destination. Knowing that most grieving people experience many of the same things they are experiencing is very reassuring and offers them a feeling of solid ground on which to stand even as so much they have known seems to be shifting and falling away.

Creating New Expressions of Grief and Healing

You are already familiar with the use of Scripture, prayer, and the sacraments as forms of pastoral care. However, as people encounter many of life's harder situations, they may need and seek other ways to express their feelings and spiritual yearnings.

Rituals have an honored history in both the Christian tradition and across all cultures. Often combining words, actions, and sacred symbols, rituals connect those who practice them with the wider human community and feed and nurture their sense of connection with the Holy. The bereaved often benefit greatly from rituals beyond that of the funeral service.

Sometimes grievers will develop their own rituals. An artist named Katherine shared her story. Her mother developed dementia, and Katherine and her brother began their grieving long before their mother's physical death. They helped her downsize and move into smaller homes, always trying to find places that would accommodate her most cherished possessions.

During these moves, and following her mother's death and interment, Katherine struggled with a particular concern: since she and her husband, Joe, do not have children, what would happen to Katherine's own beloved possessions and memories? That is, who would "inherit" Katherine's life-meanings, her spiritual legacy?

As an artist, Katherine decided to honor her own grief process and open herself to these questions by constructing what she calls "Behold!" It is a "'book-in-a-box' that emerges accordion-style in five directions from a crèche-like container. The pages contain family and cemetery photos, train tickets, the interment program, poetry, pressed flowers, a Baltimore map, journal notes, etc.... The pages are sewn and laced together, then hand-sewn into the box."[35]

For Katherine, the process of creating "Behold!" was "profound. ... Memories of the final journey for Mom were made concrete.... It has allowed me to see this other aspect of closure: my mementos, and thus Mom's mementos, go beyond the boxes into the world. The day-in, day-out creative process for 'Behold!' forced me to see and think about Mom and all the family connections and estrangements — and come to acceptance."[36]

Sometimes grievers will need your pastoral help and suggestions for developing mourning rituals. A practice as simple as lighting a candle and meditating upon their loved one can be power-fully healing. More complex rituals, perhaps involving symbolic objects like oil, stones, plants, fire, or light, and perhaps includ-ing special friends or relatives, can be fashioned to offer another level of meaning-making. The embodied aspects of rituals — touch, movement, gestures — help make the sacred incarnate and allow care-receivers to be active participants in their own restoration.

Keeping Grievers Connected

In today's culture people are too often disconnected from each other. With increasing societal mobility, many have lost their sense of community, of being truly known by others, of being in real relationship with others. This isolation causes life problems even for those who are healthy and whose lives are going well, but is even more problematic for grievers. As pastoral caregiver, you can help decrease a griever's sense of isolation both through the care you provide personally and by helping connect grievers with other social networks.

Depending on the nature of family relationships, other family members may be able to support grievers in new ways. Friends are often very willing to extend their care, especially if grievers can articulate what they need. New Internet-based networks of care resources help identify what grievers need and connect them with those in their personal relationship network who can provide for those needs.

Community organizations like Hospice often will support the bereaved, even if their loved one did not receive hospice care. Local hospitals, churches, or other agencies may offer other supports. The benefits of this are clear. People who attend support groups tend to be healthier physically, mentally, and spiritually, and to work through their grief in more constructive ways.

If you are a parish pastor, you can educate your church members about how to reach out to the bereaved. Many people are uncomfortable doing this, feeling they "don't know what to say." A workshop or church newsletter articles can help them understand what may be helpful. If your church does not offer a grief support group, you might start one. Or you might train a care team using the Stephen Minister or Called to Care models. These groups can provide helpful long-term bereavement care that you may not have time to provide. In many ways, you can help grievers build bridges with those who can best support them in your church and in the wider community.

Recognizing the Gifts

It may seem odd to think about grief as offering gifts, but it does. Those who lose a loved one often lose their own fear of death, which can lead to a sense of tremendous freedom. The bereaved may find a greater ability to discern what is truly important in life and what is not. They may become more aware of the need to nurture themselves, mentally, emotionally, and spiritually. They may also become more accepting, both of others' differences of opinions and ideas, and of life's small irritations and daily annoyances. With that acceptance, they may find a deeper sense of compassion, for others and for themselves. And in time, most bereaved people will find themselves able to reclaim joy. They will again find beauty in the world, appreciation for others, and the possibility of living a life again filled with meaning and purpose.[37]

A Last Word

I first wrote this "last word" many months ago, after the death of an especially loved parishioner who taught us all a great deal in his dying, and whose death I am still grieving. I rewrote it a few months later, when the death of another parishioner taught me some new lessons. And I rewrote it again a month ago, when still another death revealed still more about God's mystery and grace moving through these difficult experiences.

Each of those carefully crafted "last words" was as true as I could make it at the time. Each one was also incomplete. Each of those lives and each of those deaths and each of the related caregiving experiences had its own meaning and its own lessons.

And so, the last word is not mine, I think, but God's. It is a word of promise and a word of hope: the promise and the hope that our God accompanies us and those for whom we care in every circumstance, sometimes in the most profound ways. Because of that, we and our care-receivers are blessed even in times when blessings seem most unimaginable. Our lives are immeasurably deepened and enriched as those for whom we care share their tenderest and most sacred moments with us. We truly are blessed to be called to do this work. May we, in turn, be a blessing to others.

Notes

1. All Scripture citations come from the New Revised Standard Version unless noted otherwise.

2. Illustrations are drawn from my own experiences in caregiving and from those of colleagues working in various ministry settings. Names and details have been changed to preserve confidentiality for persons involved.

3. D. L. Migliore, "Death, Meaning of (Christian)," in *Dictionary of Pastoral Care and Counseling,* ed. Rodney J. Hunter (Nashville: Abingdon, 2005), 261.

4. Nelle Morton, *The Journey Is Home* (Boston: Beacon Press, 1986).

5. Alan D. Wolfelt, *Companioning the Bereaved: A Soulful Guide for Caregivers* (Ft. Collins, Colo.: Companion Press, 2006).

6. Greg Yoder, *Companioning the Dying: A Soulful Guide for Caregivers* (Fort Collins, Colo.: Companion Press, 2005).

7. Wolfelt, *Companioning the Bereaved,* 27; Yoder, *Companioning the Dying,* 11.

8. "Social location" means each person embodies a particular set of characteristics that locates them in the social world, namely, their gender, age, race, ethnicity, sexual orientation, class, occupation, etc. For example, I write from the social location of a middle-aged Euro-American ordained clergywoman in the United Church of Christ.

9. The author developed this exercise to help caregivers understand some of the losses experienced by those for whom they care.

10. Harriet Sarnoff Schiff, *The Bereaved Parent* (London: Condor, 1992), 57.

11. Kennth J. Czillinger, "Advice to Clergy on Counseling Bereaved Parents," in *Parental Loss of a Child,* ed. Therese A. Rando (Champaign, Ill.: Research Press, 1986), 468.

12. Rabbi Zalmon Schacter-Shalomi, 2000 Spring Conference of the Colorado Hospice Organization, cited in Melanie Porter, "Opal Dawn" (D.Min. diss., University of Creation Spirituality, 2005), 156.

13. D. K. Switzer, "Grief and Loss," in *Dictionary of Pastoral Care and Counseling,* ed. Rodney J. Hunter (Nashville: Abingdon, 2005), 472.

14. Susan K. Hedahl, *Listening Ministry* (Minneapolis: Fortress, 2001), 44.

15. Rainbow Spirit Elders, *Rainbow Spirit Theology* (Melbourne: HarperCollins, 1997), cited in Emmanuel Y. Lartey, *Pastoral Theology in an Intercultural World* (Cleveland: Pilgrim Press, 2006), 93.

16. Nancy J. Ramsey, ed., *Pastoral Care and Counseling: Redefining the Paradigms* (Nashville: Abingdon, 2004).

17. Lartey offers a helpful model for working with persons of cultures different from one's own. Please explore it in his book listed in the Appendix.

18. Elisabeth Kübler-Ross, *On Death and Dying* (New York: Macmillan, 1969).

19. One excellent summary of the process and a Life Review Interview Guide is in Robert G. LeFavi and Marcia H. Wessels, "Life Review in Pastoral Counseling: Background and Efficacy for Use with the Terminally Ill," *Journal of Pastoral Care and Counseling* 57 (2003).

20. Melanie Porter, hospice chaplain and former director of Spiritual Care, personal interview, March 2009, used by permission.

21. Ira Byock, *The Four Things That Matter Most* (New York: Free Press, 2004).

22. There is some debate about whether AIDS is inevitably fatal. As of this writing, the consensus is that if untreated, it is. However, in the United States, most people live many years after diagnosis if they have access to highly active antiretroviral therapy (HAART); see "AIDS," *MedlinePlus Medical Encyclopedia* nlm.nih.gov/medlineplus (accessed July 27, 2009).

23. Porter, personal interview, March 2009.

24. National Hospice and Palliative Care Organization, "NHCPO Standards of Practice" (*www.nhpco.org*, 2009).

25. "The Balancing Act: Tips for the Cancer Caregiver" (The Wellness Community, 2008), 6.

26. Porter, personal interview, March 2009.

27. Technically, during the third through ninth month after conception, the developing organism is a "fetus." For most parents-to-be, however, it is very much a "baby" or a "child." Respectfully using the same language that care-receivers use about their lost little one is important.

28. In this chapter, the term "funeral" refers to any type of after-death service. Usually at a funeral a casket and body are present; at a memorial service, they are not. Where cremation occurs, an urn containing the cremated remains ("ashes" or cremains) may be present. Most denominations do not distinguish significantly between liturgies for these different types of services.

29. Michael Blackburn, president, Callahan-Edfast Mortuary, personal interview, May 2009, used by permission.

30. The term "spouse" refers to the life-companion of the deceased, whether married or in a long-term committed relationship.

31. Erich Lindemann. "The Symptomatology and Management of Acute Grief," *American Journal of Psychiatry* 101 (September 1944): 141–48.

32. Dorothy S. Becvar, *In the Presence of Grief* (New York: Guilford, 2001), 170.

33. Ibid., 171.

34. Therese A. Rando, ed., *Parental Loss of a Child* (Champaign, Ill.: Research Press, 1986), 6.

35. Katherine Colwell, personal communication, May 2009, used by permission.

36. Ibid.

37. Becvar, *In the Presence of Grief,* 258–63.

—

Appendix

Resources for Further Reading

Anderson, Herbert, and Edward Foley. *Mighty Stories, Dangerous Rituals: Weaving Together the Human and the Divine.* San Francisco: Jossey-Bass, 2001.

Becvar, Dorothy S. *In the Presence of Grief.* New York: Guilford, 2001.

Brind, Jan, and Tessa Wilkinson. *Creative Ideas for Pastoral Liturgy — Funeral, Thanksgiving and Memorial Services.* London: Norwich, 2008.

Burnell, George M. *Freedom to Choose: How to Make End-of-Life Decisions on Your Own Terms.* Amityville, N.Y.: Baywood, 2008.

Byock, Ira. *Dying Well: The Prospect for Growth at the End of Life.* New York: Riverhead, 1998.

Cloud, Henry, and John Townsend. *Boundaries.* Grand Rapids, Mich.: Zondervan, 1992.

Coste, Joanne Koenig. *Learning to Speak Alzheimer's.* Boston: Houghton Mifflin, 2003.

Doehring, Carrie. *The Practice of Pastoral Care: A Postmodern Approach.* Louisville: Westminster John Knox Press, 2006.

Earle, Mary C. *Broken Body, Healing Spirit: Lectio Divina and Living with Illness.* Harrisburg: Morehouse, 2003.

Farris, James R. *International Perspectives on Pastoral Counseling.* New York: Haworth Press, 2002.

Fitchett, George. *Assessing Spiritual Needs.* Lima, Ohio: Academic Renewal Press, 2002.

Girard, Vickie. *There's No Place Like Hope.* Lynnwood, Wash.: Compendium, 2008.

Graham, Larry Kent. *Discovering Images of God: Narratives of Care among Lesbians and Gays.* Louisville: Westminster John Knox Press, 1997.

Heydahl, Susan K. *Listening Ministry: Rethinking Pastoral Leadership.* Minneapolis: Fortress, 2001.

Hodge, David R. *Spiritual Assessment: A Handbook for Helping Professionals.* Botsford, Conn.: North American Association of Christians in Social Work, 2003.

Kirkwood, Neville. *A Hospital Handbook on Multiculturalism and Religion.* Harrisburg: Morehouse, 2005.

Kuenning, Delores. *Helping People through Grief.* Minneapolis: Bethany House, 1987.

Lartey, Emmanuel Y. *Pastoral Theology in an Intercultural World.* Cleveland: Pilgrim Press, 2006.

London, Eileen, and Belinda Recio. *Sacred Rituals: Connecting with Spirit through Labyrinths, Sand Paintings and Other Traditional Arts.* Gloucester: Fair Winds Press, 2004.

McCall, Junietta Baker. *Bereavement Counseling.* New York: Haworth Pastoral Press, 2004.

McEwan, Dorothea, Pat Pinsent, Ianthe Pratt, and Veronica Seddon, eds. *Making Liturgy: Creating Rituals for Worship and Life.* Cleveland: Pilgrim Press, 2001.

McFarlane, Doreen M. *Funerals with Today's Families in Mind.* Cleveland: Pilgrim Press, 2008.

Melander, Rochelle, and Harold Eppley. *The Spiritual Leader's Guide to Self-Care.* Washington, D.C.: Alban Institute, 2002.

Migliore, Daniel L. *Faith Seeking Understanding.* Grand Rapids, Mich.: Eerdmans, 2004.

Norberg, Tilda. *Gathered Together: Creating Personal Liturgies for Healing and Transformation.* Nashville: Upper Room, 2007.

Patton, John. *Pastoral Care: An Essential Guide.* Nashville: Abingdon, 2005.

———. *Pastoral Care in Context.* Lousville: John Knox, 2005.

Peterson, Sharyl B. *The Indispensable Guide to Pastoral Care.* Cleveland: Pilgrim Press, 2008.

Purnell, Douglas. *Conversation as Ministry.* Cleveland: Pilgrim Press, 2003.

Ramsey, Nancy, ed. *Pastoral Care and Counseling: Redefining the Paradigms.* Nashville: Abingdon, 2004.

Ramshaw, Elaine. *Ritual and Pastoral Care.* Philadelphia: Fortress, 1987.

Rando, Theresa A., ed. *Parental Loss of a Child.* Champaign, Ill.: Research Press, 1986.

Rupp, Joyce. *Praying Our Goodbyes.* Notre Dame, Ind.: Ave Maria, 2009.

Schiff, Harriet Sarnoff. *The Bereaved Parent.* London: Condor, 1992.

Stone, Howard W. *How to Think Theologically.* Minneapolis: Fortress, 2006.

———. *Theological Context for Pastoral Caregiving: Word in Deed.* Binghamton, N.Y.: Haworth Pastoral Press, 1996.

Sunderland, Ronald H. *AIDS: A Manual for Pastoral Care.* Lousville: Westminster, 1987.

Vennard, Jane E. *Praying with Body and Soul.* Minneapolis: Augsburg Fortress, 1998.

Westberg, Granger E. *Good Grief.* Philadelphia: Fortress, 2004.

Wolfelt, Alan D. *Companioning the Bereaved.* Fort Collins, Colo.: Companion Press, 2006.

Yoder, Greg. *Companioning the Dying.* Fort Collins, Colo.: Companion Press, 2005.